New Light
at
the Cape of Good Hope:

William Porter: The Father of Cape Liberalism

GW00683723

NEW LIGHT
at the
CAPE
of
GOOD HOPE

◆

WILLIAM PORTER
The Father of Cape Liberalism

◆

J. L. McCracken

ULSTER HISTORICAL FOUNDATION
PUBLICATIONS

To
Seán, Donal and Dermot McCracken
and
Colin, Victoria and Sara Louise McCracken

Published 1993 by
The Ulster Historical Foundation
12 College Square East, Belfast BT1 6DD

© J. L. McCracken 1993

ISBN 0-901905-54-2

Typeset by the Ulster Historical Foundation
Printed by the Universities Press, Alanbrooke Road, Belfast.

The Belfast Natural History and Philosophical Society assisted
with the costs of publishing this book.

*Cover illustrations: Portrait of William Porter by F. Wolf reproduced
by kind permission of the Library of Parliament, Cape Town; painting of
Heerengracht c.1840 reproduced by kind permission of the
Africana Museum, Johannesburg*

Design by Wendy Dunbar

Contents

List of Illustrations

Abbreviations

Preface

It is strange that the man with the best claim to being regarded as the father of Cape liberalism has been so neglected by historians and has not attracted a biographer earlier. In general histories and specialised monographs alike he is either not mentioned at all or is dismissed in a sentence or two, often so worded as to reveal a minimal acquaintance with the man and his career. Two factors have probably contributed to this state of affairs. William Porter's years in South Africa were indeed eventful and significant but they lacked the dramatic and emotive qualities of what came before and after: they fell between the Great Trek and the discovery of diamonds and gold, both rich in men and events calculated to capture the historian's attention to the detriment of a more placid age. A more positive deterrent to a study of Porter is the dearth of material and its dispersal. No substantial body of personal papers has survived — most likely it never existed — so an examination of his life and work has to be based on a wide variety of miscellaneous sources in Ireland, Britain and South Africa. The effort is worthwhile. The liberalism which took root at the Cape in Porter's day was to fade before powerful new political and economic forces and changed ideologies and values. But it did not wither away; enough survived to make the liberal tradition a significant component of South African public life and to justify a study of its origins.

William Porter was one of the many nineteenth-century Irishmen who served the crown in every corner of the British empire. The Cape Colony had had its share of Irish governors, soldiers and officials but when Porter became the colony's second attorney general in 1839 a new breed of Irishman joined their ranks.

He was the first Irish liberal to occupy high office in the colony. His background, experiences and outlook were different from those of Irishmen like Sir Galbraith Lowry Cole, who had been governor a few years before his time, or Captain R. T. Wolfe, commandant of Robben Island, who welcomed him on his arrival. They belonged to the Irish landed-gentry class, the privileged minority which upheld the episcopal state church and monopolised political power and influence. Porter had a middle class, nonconformist background which hitherto had been a bar to official preferment. He owed his appointment to a temporary accord between Lord Melbourne's whig government and the Irish Catholic leader, Daniel O'Connell.

Porter was not merely a liberal, he was an Irish liberal, as distinct from a British liberal as he was from his fellow countrymen at the Cape. Irish liberals, it is true, identified themselves with British liberal causes and policies, but they were exposed to experiences alien to their British counterparts, for Irish society was sharply divided on ethnic, religious and political grounds. Porter imbibed his liberalism from the New Light, a small heterodox movement within the Presbyterian church in Ireland, whose adherents held advanced theological views and took a liberal stand on political issues, including the emancipation of Catholics, the most controversial issue of the day in Ireland.

For thirty-four years Porter used his position at the Cape to promote liberal ideals. He strove to enforce equality before the law and the suppression of white injustices against blacks. Without prompting from the colonial office he included in the constitution he drafted for the colony provisions which enabled men of colour to participate in parliamentary elections, and he resolutely defended his colour-blind franchise against attack from all quarters. He deprecated the condescending or contemptuous attitude of many English-speaking colonists towards the Dutch-speaking section of the population and he acquired a working knowledge of Dutch himself. He deplored sectarian bitterness and exclusiveness. He supported the demand for responsible

9

government while he was still an official, in opposition to the wishes of the governor, and he was the first to be offered the newly created position of prime minister in 1872.

Porter came to occupy a position of great influence. His unprecedented tenure of the same key office for so long made him the repository of knowledge and experience which governors, colonial secretaries and colonial office officials were glad to draw upon. The esteem in which he was held at the Cape was such that even those who did not share his convictions respected his opinions; no better instance can be cited than the hearing accorded to him when he introduced in the house of assembly in 1870 a bill to abolish capital punishment. The element of liberalism in Cape public life which was still a reality when the colony was merged in the Union of South Africa owed much to the principles and example of William Porter. As Professor Phyllis Lewson has said, 'the strength of liberalism was much less a matter of numbers than of the calibre of its adherents and their role in Cape affairs'.[1] Porter is the outstanding claimant to that position of prominence in the formative years of the Cape liberal tradition.

1 P. Lewson, 'The Cape liberal tradition — myth or reality' in *Institute for the study of man in Africa. Paper No. 26*, November 1969.

Acknowledgements

Many years ago Mrs Helen McKay, then caring for manuscripts in the Gubbins Collection of the University of the Witwatersrand, laid upon me the obligation of attempting to win proper recognition for my countryman, William Porter, whom she described as the finest man who ever held office in the Cape Colony. To her I am indebted for having inspired the project. For its ultimate completion I have to thank Rhodes University which, by appointing me to the Hugh Le May Fellowship, enabled me to devote a year's research to the South African sources not available to me in Ireland or Britain. In the intervening years I have become beholden to many people for lending me documents, pointing me to sources, sharing their specialist knowledge, patiently submitting to interrogation and being generous with stimulating ideas, encouragement and hospitality.

I have had the privilege of meeting members of both the Porter and the Classon families. Without their help it would have been impossible to piece together an outline of Porter's career, let alone attempt to assess his character and significance. Mrs Margot Vernon, the senior member of the family in Ireland at the time, remembered her great-uncle though not very clearly, for she was only six when he died in 1880. She was an inspiring source of information and a most gifted and generous communicator of it. Equally willing to help and equally kind and hospitable was Mr Eric Porter, also of Dublin. Mr Basil Porter of Port Elizabeth, descended from William's half-brother Classon, was as helpful and as generous as the Irish branch of the family. From Rev. Michael Classon and his aunt Miss Nora Classon I

11

received invaluable assistance and great hospitality. I wish to record my sincere thanks to all of them.

Work done sporadically over many years has incurred for me a debt of gratitude to many staff in the great national libraries and repositories — the National Library of Ireland, the British Library, the South African Library, the Library of Parliament, Cape Town, the Public Record Office, London, the Public Record Office of Northern Ireland, the Cape Archives Depot - and in smaller libraries, Magee College Library, University of Ulster at Londonderry, the Linenhall Library, Belfast, the Cory Library, Rhodes University, the Killie Campbell Library, Durban and the Don Africana Library, Durban. I am most grateful for the help I received.

Finally, I should like to mention some people who have, at one time or another, been specially helpful to me: T. McCallum Walker, Nance McCauley, John MacMaster, W. S. Ferguson, Alan Roberts, all in Londonderry; in Belfast, Brian Trainor, James Vitty and Aiken McClelland who produced a single letter which held the key to Porter's career; John Brown, guide, philosopher and friend, if ever there was; Richard Hawkins, who threw light on Lynar; W. J. de Kock, first editor-in-chief of the *South African Dictionary of Biography*, whose visit to Ireland not only cemented a valued friendship but resulted in the South African Library acquiring important Porter papers; Dr Keith Hunt who masterminded my return to South Africa; Mike Berning, Sandy Fold and Tyrell Glynn who smoothed my path in South African libraries.

SOURCES AND ACKNOWLEDGEMENTS FOR ILLUSTRATIONS

Portrait of William Porter by F. Wolf, by kind permission of the Library of Parliament, Cape Town; Porter in his uniform as captain of the Cape Volunteer Army, *Cape Monthly Magazine*, vol. V. 1859; portrait of Hugh Lynar, by kind permission of the Cape Archives Depot, Cape Town; photograph of John Classon, copy provided by Rev. Michael Classon; photograph of Adam Kok, reproduced by kind permission of the Cape Archives Depot, Cape Town; advertisement for Artillery Lane School, reproduced from the *Londonderry Journal*, 18 July 1820, by kind permission of Mrs Moore; photograph of 2 Blackhall Place, copy provided by the author; Northumberland Hotel, reproduced from *Irish Transport and General Workers Union – Fifty Years of Liberty Hall* (Dublin 1959); King's Inns, Dublin, reproduced by kind permission of the National Library of Ireland; Four Courts, Dublin, from *Dublin Penny Journal*, I. 141. 27 X 1832 reproduced by kind permission of the University of Durban Westville Library; Kingstown pier, reproduced from *Dublin Penny Journal*, II. 233. 25 I 1834 reproduced by kind permission of the University of Durban Westville Library; advertisement for the *Sterling*, reproduced from *South African Commercial Advertiser*, 9 X 1839; Heerengracht, Cape Town, c. 1840, by courtesy of the Africana Museum, Johannesburg; St George's Street, Cape Town in the 1840s, reproduced from E. Delessert, *Voyages dans deux océans, 1844 and 1847*, by courtesy of the Don Africana Library, Durban; Wolmunster, photograph provided by the author; Old Supreme Court, Cape Town, reproduced by kind permission of the Library of Parliament, Cape Town; Colesburg, reproduced from Gustav Fritsch, *Drei jahre in Süd Afrika*, (Breslau, 1868), p. 240 by the Africana Museum, Johannesburg; Phillipolis, reproduced from James Backhouse, *A narrative of a visit to the Mauritius and South Africa*, p. 349 by the Africana Museum, Johannesburg; Cradock Kloof Pass in 1840, by kind permission of the Africana Museum, Johannesburg; anti-convict meeting at the Commercial Exchange, by kind permission of the Africana Museum, Johannesburg; opening ceremony of the the first Cape Parliament, reproduced from the *Illustrated London News*, 16 September 1854 by the Don Africana Library, Durban; Banqueting Hall, Goede Hoop Masonic Lodge, by kind permission of the Library of Parliament, Cape Town; Opening of Parliament, Grahamstown, 1864, reproduced from the *Illustrated London News*, 16 July 1864 by the Don Africana Library, Durban.

Maps of Ireland, the Cape in 1839 and 1873 were drawn by Gill Alexander, Queen's University of Belfast.

PART 1

The road to the Cape

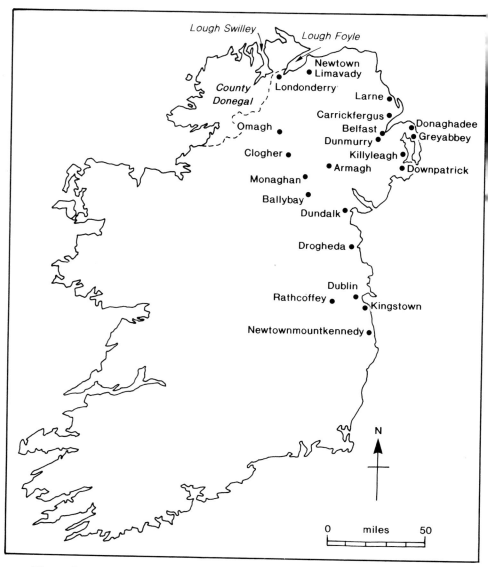

Places in Ireland associated with William Porter and the Porter family.

1

The Formative Years

William Porter was born into a colonial situation. When Ireland's northernmost province of Ulster was being colonised by settlers from England and Scotland at the beginning of the seventeenth century, an extensive area in the valley of the river Roe was granted to an English soldier of fortune, Sir Thomas Phillips. The dispossessed Irish clan, the O'Cahans, had a castle at Leim a Mhadaidh (Dog's Leap), some ten kilometres from the river's mouth in Lough Foyle on the north coast. In the vicinity of the old castle Phillips began building the town of Newtownlimavady in 1612 for the British settlers he was bringing over to found his colony. By the beginning of the nineteenth century it had become a thriving little market town with a fertile hinterland inhabited by Protestant planters of English and Scottish descent and a mountainous fringe occupied by the native Catholic Irish. Two miles away, in the townland of Artikelly, William Porter was born on Sunday 15 September 1805.

He was the third child and second son of Rev. William Porter, Presbyterian minister of Limavady, by his first wife, Mary Scott. When he was four years old his mother died and a year and a half later his father married his second wife, Eliza Classon. The two families, his own and his stepmother's, had equal shares in shaping Porter's character, ideals and destiny. They had much in common. Both were of settler stock, but not of the privileged, landowning aristocracy; both had attained their position in society by the prized liberal virtue of self-help in the face of discrimination and adversity; both belonged to a minority community with heterodox religious beliefs and liberal political convictions.

The Porters were northern Irish Presbyterians, dating back to the seventeenth-century Plantation of Ulster. Two of the original settler's sons established themselves in Co. Donegal, in the north-west of the province, the third in the Ulster midland county of Tyrone where, in the eighteenth century, his descendants were farmers at Cranny, about a mile from the town of Omagh. It was here that William Porter's father was born in 1774 to John Porter and his second wife Jane Nixon, the daughter of a neighbouring farmer. He had the odd experience of receiving part of his early education in Omagh gaol: his first teacher was arrested for debt and while he was in prison he was allowed to carry on the school within the gaol. For his more advanced schooling Porter was sent to Rev. Andrew Millar, Presbyterian minister of Clogher, Co. Tyrone, who took in a few boarders and had the reputation of giving them a sound classical and mathematical education. After about two years at this school Porter entered Glasgow University in November 1791. This was the normal course for young Ulster Presbyterians who aspired to join the ministry of their church. No facilities for higher education were available to them in Ireland because Ireland's only university, the University of Dublin, was an Anglican institution. Since public transport was meagre and expensive, youths like Porter were obliged to make their way on foot to an east coast port, usually Donaghadee, and there find a passage on a trading vessel to Portpatrick or some other Scottish port, from where they walked to Glasgow. The university session at Glasgow lasted from November till May, but what with delays on the journey from home, difficulties in getting a passage, and contrary winds the Irish students were often late in arriving. Frequently, too, they had to leave before the end of the session because their resources ran out.

For some reason that is not known Porter missed a session and did not take his degree until April 1795. Instead of proceeding with his theological studies at Glasgow he then went to the University of Edinburgh. The reason was that his father had heard disturbing reports about the heterodox views held by some of the professors at Glasgow and being a strict Calvinist he did not want his son to be corrupted. In the event, his precautions were in vain. Porter spent two years at Edinburgh completing his theological training. In May 1797 he entered on a probationary period under the presbytery of Strabane before being licensed in the following August. He was then a licentiate, a man declared qualified to take charge of a congregation but without a congregation of his own.

This state of affairs lasted for two years during which time he was employed in filling the vacancy in congregations without a minister or in preaching for ministers who needed assistance. The work entailed moving about the country and for this purpose his father supplied him with a good horse. It was a way of life that brought him into contact with a great many people and gave him ample experience of preaching. During these two years the country was profoundly disturbed by the activities of the United Irishmen who eventually launched a rebellion in 1798. The turmoil may have contributed to the delay in establishing Porter in a congregation but a more immediate cause was his own unorthodox beliefs. The Arianism which was to become increasingly pronounced was already sufficiently evident to make him unacceptable to many congregations. After preaching for four Sundays at Ballybay, Co. Monaghan, which was then vacant, he refused to allow a vote to be taken on his candidature because, he said, there was only one man in the entire congregation who would vote for him. When he preached the same sermon at Limavady some time later, however, he had a very different reception; he received a unanimous vote of approval. On 1 August 1799 he was ordained to the charge of the Limavady congregation and there he remained for the rest of his life. Just over a month later, on 24 September, he married his cousin Mary, the daughter of John Scott, a farmer neighbour and brother-in-law of his father.

Unlike many Presbyterians, neither Rev. William Porter nor his family was involved in the United Irish conspiracy or the

1798 rebellion. His brother James, who inherited the home farm at Cranny as well as the farm of their grandfather Nixon, was an officer in the pro-government yeomanry and Porter himself was chaplain to the Limavady corps of volunteers at the time of the threatened French invasion in 1805. But if his political loyalty was beyond reproach his doctrinal orthodoxy was suspect among a good many of his fellow ministers. Nevertheless, his reputation for ability and integrity was such that when the clerkship of the General Synod of Ulster[1] fell vacant in 1816 he was elected to the office after he had conducted a province-wide canvass of the ministers. In addition to carrying a salary of £50 a year this office brought Porter considerable influence, for it put him in close touch with all the congregations attached to the synod. Licentiates were eager to preach before him because they knew that he was in a position to help them find a congregation. His professional assistance was sought even by clergymen of other denominations and he was once asked for the loan of some of his sermons by a curate of the Church of Ireland, 'who, conscious of his own inadequacy, knows where the ability is, and trusts to the kindness of one more competent than himself'.

Porter was at the heart of the controversy between the orthodox majority and the Arian, or New Light, group within the Presbyterian church. He had, as we have seen, made no secret of his views for a long time, but when he told the commissioners of Irish Education Inquiry in Belfast in October 1825, 'I set out in life with orthodox sentiments and I am now what is usually called an Arian', and asserted that there were more real Arians than professed ones in the synod[2] he infuriated the orthodox party and became a target for their attacks. Repeated efforts were made to oust him from the clerkship and when a split in the church came in 1829 he and his congregation were among the seceders. In May 1830 he was elected first moderator of the Remonstrant Synod, the governing body of the Unitarians, and in September 1831 he was appointed clerk of that body, an office which he held till his death in 1843. Like other New Light leaders Porter was liberal in his politics, and respected by liberals outside his own religious community. At the height of the Arian controversy he was presented with a silver service by his friends 'of the different denominations' in Limavady as a tribute to his defence of the right of private judgement.[3]

All Porter's children adhered to the New Light principles that he adopted. Apart from William and his youngest stepbrother Francis who was to follow him to the Cape all the sons became Unitarian ministers: John Scott in Belfast, Classon in Larne, Co. Antrim and James Nixon in Carrickfergus, Co. Antrim and later in Warrington in England. A daughter married Frank Dalzell Finlay, founder of the *Northern Whig*, the Belfast newspaper which spoke for Ulster liberalism. Finlay, who wanted Belfast to have 'a free press; a press that no man shall call servant, and that will acknowledge no master but the law' was once gaoled for three months for refusing to reveal the author of an allegedly libellous letter.[4] His devotion to liberalism is reflected in the naming of his sons; Porter's father once wryly remarked, 'Finlay's sons are all designated by highly illustrious appellations'[5] — George Washington, Henry Montgomery, Hamilton Rowan. Of the clerical sons the most distinguished was John Scott Porter. After spending six years in London as minister of Carter Lane Chapel in the City of London he returned to Belfast where he was, for the rest of his life, a leading Unitarian divine, a professor of Hebrew and theology for non-subscribing divinity students, a prolific exponent of Unitarian doctrine and a notable public figure. It was to his home that William Porter returned, after thirty-four years at the Cape, to spend the closing years of his life.[6]

The other family to which William Porter was deeply indebted was the Classon family of Dublin, his stepmother's family. Like the Porters, the Classons were Presbyterians with Arian leanings but their background was different. The first Classon in Ireland was a soldier in William III's army who was given a substantial grant of land in Co. Wicklow at the end of the war. His descendant, John Classon, Eliza Classon's father, was a man of greater wealth and higher social standing than the Porters. He had a country house on his estate near Newtownmountkennedy in Co. Wicklow, a town house in Eustace Street, Dublin, and large dye-stuff mills at Palmerston, near Dublin. His wife, Hester Andrews, the daughter of a wealthy Dublin brewer, was a woman of strong character and lively mind. In her old age she claimed that she had 'never tasted water unadulterated in all her life'. But misfortune befell the family. When John Classon was driving into Dublin from his country seat one day his carriage-horses bolted and he was so severely injured about the head that he was never able to attend to his business again. His wife did her best to take his place, for all the children were young, but when he died not long after the accident his affairs were found to be in such a state that the family had to adapt itself to a much reduced scale of living. The Wicklow property was lost, the sons had to be sent to a cheap school in Yorkshire where, it is said, they were nearly starved, and some of the daughters had to go out as governesses. Such was the fate of Eliza. She went as governess to the family of Mrs Archibald Hamilton Rowan who lived partly in Dublin and partly at Rathcoffey, Co. Kildare and Killyleagh, Co. Down. Hamilton Rowan himself at this time was in exile, on the continent or in America, following his involvement in the United Irish conspiracy. After a spell as governess Eliza went to Londonderry as assistant in a school kept by a Mrs Graham. Shortly afterwards she succeeded Mrs Graham and with the help of her younger sister Fanny she ran a large boarding and day school for girls for some years until her marriage. It was while she was teaching in Londonderry, which is 30 kilometres from Limavady, that Eliza Classon chanced to hear of William Porter's mother, who was so seriously ill that she had been placed under the care of a Doctor Caldwell in the town and was living alone in lodgings. Taking pity on the invalid, she called and got into the habit of visiting regularly and reading to her in the evenings after school. A warm friendship developed and the first Mrs Porter declared that she would die happy if she thought that her children would be brought up by her friend. In due course her wish was fulfilled; on 13 April 1811 Eliza Classon was married to Rev. William Porter by Rev. George Hay, one of the Presbyterian ministers in Londonderry, and a co-founder of a classical school in the town to which William Porter was subsequently sent.[7]

The Classon family fortunes were substantially repaired by Eliza's brother, John Classon, an iron and timber merchant in Dublin. The firm of Classon and Duggan had premises in Bridgefoot Street and at 2 Blackhall Place, where Classon lived. He built on Eden Quay the Northumberland Buildings which housed stalls for the sale of fruit and other goods, offices, a weighbridge, a bath-house and a chop house. He also built the Northumberland Hotel in Beresford Place.[8] As a prosperous Dublin merchant Classon had the resources to advance William Porter's career in a way that a poor Presbyterian minister like his father could never have done.

1 The governing body of the Presbyterian church in Ulster.
2 *Fourth report of commission of Irish Education Inquiry*, H.C. 1826-7, xiii (89) pp.136-7.
3 *NW*, 29 December 1827.
4 C. O'Byrne, *As I roved out*, p.186.
5 Rev. William Porter to Hugh Lynar, 16 March 1841, SAL. Porter papers.
6 C. Porter, *Irish Presbyterian biographical sketches; memorial addresses and sermons, Rev. J. S. Porter and Hon. W. Porter.*
7 MS note on Classon family by Rev. Classon Porter. In possession of Rev. Michael Classon.
8 In 1912 the Northumberland Hotel became the headquarters of the Irish Transport and General Workers Union and the name was changed to Liberty Hall. It was a focal point in the Irish rising of 1916.

2

The Irish Apprenticeship

William Porter was thirty-four years of age when he was appointed attorney general of the Cape Colony. For all the years he lived in Ireland the country was torn by strife and tension. The year of his birth, 1805, was a crisis year. For most of it the threat of a massive French invasion hung over Britain and then, in the latter part of the year, her European allies suffered defeat at the hands of Napoleon, leaving Britain in isolation. An invasion scare was nothing new to Ireland, for on five occasions between 1793 and 1798 French expeditions had been planned or dispatched against the country. The far north of Ireland was as apprehensive as anywhere else in 1805, recent events having shown that remoteness gave it no immunity. In October 1798 a French fleet which had sailed the length of the western seaboard was intercepted off the coast of Donegal in the north-west, and a ship of the line, the *Hoche*, was captured and brought into Lough Swilly, some 40 kilometres from the Porter home. To meet the new danger, coastal defences were hurriedly put in hand and a volunteer force was mobilised. Porter's father was chaplain of the Limavady corps of volunteers and in a sermon[1] delivered to the corps in his own church during the invasion scare he reflected the public anxiety:

> Picture to yourselves the dreadful consequences even of the temporary success of our enemies. Can you think without horror of seeing your native village reduced to ashes, in order to make room for a battlefield more destructive than the flames, the male inhabitants slaughtered in one day of carnage, and their distracted families seeking in vain for their mangled remains, or weeping in fearful silence over the smoking ruins of their desolated dwellings.

In face of such a potential disaster he called upon his listeners to form, 'a band of brothers.... Let jealousy and strife be banished from your ranks.'

A similar plea to a wider audience would not have been out of place, for brotherliness was not conspicuous in the Ireland of the day. There were those, even within Porter's own religious group, who would have welcomed a successful French invasion. A turbulent history had endowed the country with a society sharply divided by barriers of race, religion and class. The dominant minority of landowners were British in origin and outlook, and Anglican in religion; the great mass of the Catholic Irish, still largely Irish-speaking, were tenants or labourers on the estates of this Protestant aristocracy; the Protestant population of the north, to which the Porters belonged, was made up largely of tenant farmers, merchants and tradesmen, mainly of Scottish descent and predominantly Presbyterian in religion. Longstanding enmities between the groups lay at the root of the 1798 rebellion in which both Catholics and Presbyterians were involved. To the British government, immersed in the war with revolutionary France, the best hope for British security and Irish stability appeared to lie in a closer union of the two kingdoms. The Act of Union of 1800 abolished the Irish parliament and brought into being the United Kingdom of Great Britain and Ireland.

The union brought neither peace nor prosperity to Ireland. The fears and prejudices of the landowning class had been deeply stirred by the rebellion of 1798 and the abortive rising of Robert Emmet in 1803. They saw their ascendancy, and even their survival, threatened by a politically disgruntled Catholic middle class and a militant Catholic peasantry. Though they continued to monopolise public office they were alarmed by the decline in their political influence since the demise of the Irish parliament and they resented the whig and radical criticism to which they were subjected in the United Kingdom parliament. They had little confidence in the ability of United Kingdom governments to manage Irish affairs to their liking but they realised that the union was vital to their interests and that they had no choice but to support it. They were resolved, however, to resist vigorously any further encroachment on their privileged position, even by their fellow Protestants, the northern Presbyterians.

The Catholic bishops and the Catholic middle class were aggrieved because the union had not been followed by Catholic emancipation, the granting of full civil and political rights to Roman Catholics. The Catholic peasantry were bitter and restive in the aftermath of the rebellion. Their numbers were increasing rapidly, and in a country without the natural resources to sustain an industrial revolution the population explosion was putting increased pressure on the land, leading to the subdivision of farms, soaring rents and unemployment. Furthermore, the Catholic Irish were obliged to pay tithes for the upkeep of the Protestant state church, the Church of Ireland, in addition to supporting their own clergy. The outcome was an upsurge of agrarian violence conducted by peasant secret societies concerned with economic grievances like land shortage, high rents and tithes. In the north the violence took the form of sectarian conflict between the Catholic Ribbonmen and the Protestant Orangemen. Different parts of the country were affected at different times but from 1801 until the 1840s, that is to say for the whole span of William Porter's life in Ireland, violence was endemic.

The third major component of Irish society, the Presbyterians of the north, entered the post-union era disillusioned with the radicalism which had led some of them into futile rebellion. With the decline of radicalism came a revival of their traditional enmity towards the Catholic Irish and a growing acceptance by them of the union. Communal bitterness dated back to the seventeenth-century colonisation of Ulster but a new development was the strengthening of Ulster's economic ties with Britain. Unlike the rest of Ireland, the north became industrialised in the early decades of the nineteenth century and Belfast developed along the lines of an English industrial city. In these circumstances many northern Presbyterians came to regard the political union as the mainstay of their economic well-being. Their reaction from the radicalism of the late eighteenth century, with its republican and nationalist aspirations and its revolutionary leanings, was further stimulated by an evangelical revival within their ranks.

Not all Presbyterians, however, participated in this conservative revival. What took the place of radicalism among a few of the northern Protestant colonists was a liberalism which broadly followed its British counterpart in ideology and political programme. It drew its support mainly from the middle class, which was largely Presbyterian, and its views found expression in the Belfast newspaper, the *Northern Whig*, founded in 1824 by Francis Dalzell Finlay who married William Porter's sister Mary Ann in 1830. The *Northern Whig* supported Catholic emancipation, parliamentary reform, the abolition of slavery and the repeal of the corn laws; it denounced the evils of Irish landlordism; it attacked the Church of Ireland and demanded the abolition of tithes; it advocated joint education of Catholic and Protestant children so that they might learn that:

> rational and genuine piety is the property of no particular sect but that the rays of true religion while they contain an assemblage of distinct colours ... afford light and heat to the world by their intimate coalescence.

But critical though it was of the Irish establishment the *Whig* accepted the union, dismissing repeal as romantic and impracticable. In a wider sphere it came out, for example, on the side of the Greeks in their struggle for independence, and it speculated on the extent to which the Boers' sufferings at the hands of the Zulus were the outcome of their own transgressions. The Ulster liberals supported the British whig party, unlike the majority of northern Presbyterians who were firm adherents of the tory party.[2]

In the midst of all this dissent William Porter grew up in a happy household. When Eliza Classon married Rev. William Porter in 1811 she became stepmother to his four children by his first wife. In due course she was to have four children of her own. The confidence of the first Mrs Porter in the friend of her dying days was well-founded: Eliza made no distinction between her own children and her stepchildren, and she always urged her husband to give the first family the best education he could afford in the conviction that they would help the second family. William Porter, towards the end of his life, described her as 'an excellent woman who never made the least difference between my mother's children and her own', and his half-brother Classon said that he never knew they were not all the children of the same mother until he was a youth at college.[3]

There were several small schools in Limavady supported by their pupils' fees. It was to one of these that William Porter was sent for his earliest education. The school was run by a Presbyterian schoolmaster called James Stephenson in an 'indifferent' schoolhouse reckoned to have cost £20. From the twenty or so pupils the master drew a total annual income of about £14.[4] From this humble establishment Porter proceeded to a school in Artillery Lane, Londonderry, attended also by his elder brother, John Scott. This school was established about 1810 by two Presbyterian ministers, Rev. George Hay and Rev. William Moore.

It is indicative of the change of heart among Presbyterians in the early years of the nineteenth century that while George Hay's father, a schoolmaster in Larne, Co. Antrim, had been imprisoned in Carrickfergus gaol during the 1798 rebellion and had had his house wrecked and burned by government supporters, Hay himself eventually became government agent for the distribution of the state grant to Presbyterian ministers.[5] The school in Artillery Lane was founded to provide an education for Presbyterians because the existing grammar school in Londonderry was a Church of Ireland establishment, dominated by the bishop of Derry. In addition to such subjects as bookkeeping, navigation and surveying which would equip pupils for a mercantile career, the Artillery Lane school offered Latin and Greek like the stock classical grammar school, for those intending to enter a profession. That was the career designed for the elder brother, John Scott, but the family resources did not permit further education for the second son; instead, William was apprenticed to his stepmother's brother, John Classon, in Dublin.

While Porter was serving his apprenticeship in Dublin, Daniel O'Connell launched his great crusade for Catholic emancipation. Until its successful outcome in 1829 rural violence subsided over the Catholic parts of the country for O'Connell enrolled the peasantry in the Catholic Association and inspired them with the belief that emancipation was the panacea for all their ills. But his campaign greatly intensified sectarian bitterness. 'Never', wrote the chief secretary in 1826, 'were Roman Catholics and Protestants so decidedly distinguished and opposed'.[6] The landed gentry and the rank and file of northern Protestants were vehemently opposed to emancipation and the ultra-Protestant Orange Order took on a new lease of life. Protestants like Porter's father who supported emancipation and abhorred sectarian strife were very much in the minority.

Concurrently with the emancipation campaign, a politico-religious crisis was developing within the Presbyterian church. Radicalism had been widespread among the Presbyterian ministers in the closing years of the eighteenth century. Some twenty of them were implicated in the 1798 rebellion and one, Rev. James Porter of Greyabbey, Co. Down, a distant relative of the Limavady Porters, was hanged before his manse because of his involvement with the dissidents.[7] Immediately after the rising, the General Synod of Ulster condemned the conduct of the disaffected ministers and this prepared the way for an arrangement with the government under which the state grant to the Presbyterian ministers was substantially increased in a bid to ensure Presbyterian loyalty.

The swing to conservatism in the synod and the spread of an evangelical revival among Presbyterians combined to bring to a head a long-standing cleavage within the Presbyterian church between the orthodox majority, the Old Light party, who demanded subscription to the 1643 Westminister Confession of Faith from all candidates for the Presbyterian ministry, and a heterodox minority, the New Light party, who held various doctrines on the Trinity, ranging from Arianism to Unitarianism,[8] and who opposed the principle of subscription to any rigid creed. New Light supporters, being more intellectual and less emotional in their approach to religion, tended to be drawn from the better educated and more prosperous elements in society; the Old Light party could count on the support of the masses, where evangelicalism had greater appeal. The division extended to political convictions; the Old Light party identified itself with conservative politics, the New Light party championed liberal causes. On the burning issue of the day, Catholic emancipation, the conflicting stances were clearly revealed. Old Light leaders opposed emancipation with varying degrees of intensity. New Light leaders, like Porter's father and his friend Rev. Henry Montgomery, were dedicated supporters. Montgomery went so far as to attend a meeting in the New Chapel, Belfast, presided over by Dr William Crolly, Catholic bishop of Down and Connor, and to speak from the altar, urging Catholics to continue their agitation until they succeeded in their campaign.[9] Porter's father, as we have seen, had been an avowed Arian since his student days and when the struggle between the two parties in the church grew in intensity in the 1820s he was the central figure in the conflict. Its outcome was the withdrawal of the non-subscribers from the Synod of Ulster in 1829 and the formation of a new body called the Remonstrant Synod of Ulster. In 1825, by which time William Porter was taking a hand in the controversy, the Remonstrant Synod united with two other Presbyterian groups which shared its Arian principles, the

30

Presbytery of Antrim and the Synod of Munster,[10] to form the Association of Non-subscribing Presbyterians in Ireland.

The New Light controversy was just building up to its climax when Rev. William Porter received a disturbing letter.[11] His son was not a success in business. According to Frances Classon, John Classon's unmarried sister, known in the family as Aunt Fanny, every day brought fresh proof of William's unfitness for business. He had had to give up keeping the books at Blackhall Place and when he was cashier for a short time at Bridgefoot Street matters got 'rather out of order'. He had no interest in his work and no heart in it. If he stayed in the office he would only be an encumbrance. She was writing in March 1826, when William's apprenticeship was within a few months of its end. And she had a plan for his future. All William's inclinations were literary and historical, he was well-informed on politics and general subjects, he had clear judgment and was an eloquent public speaker. He had recently made a mark by his speech at an historical society to which he belonged on the question 'Was Coriolanus justifiable in retiring from before Rome at the entreaties of his wife and mother?' All these facts, in her mind, pointed in one direction, the law, and she had her brother's full support. Her plan was that William should finish his apprenticeship but at the same time he should take up classical studies under Dr Drummond. He could attend to the office a few hours in the forenoon and have plenty of time for study in the morning and evening. His uncle would cover his expenses while he remained in Ireland, which would be until the autumn when he would enter the Temple. In London he could economise by living with his brother John Scott who had just been installed as minister of Carter Lane Chapel in the City, but the expenses of his legal studies would be borne by his uncle. The scheme was entirely of Aunt Fanny's devising; not a word of it was to be disclosed to William until his father's approval was secured. The plan proved to be acceptable to all concerned and it was adopted almost in its entirety.

The Dr Drummond with whom William was to read the classics was William Hamilton Drummond, one of the ministers of Strand Street Presbyterian church in Dublin, a graduate of Glasgow and a Doctor of Divinity of Aberdeen. He was a scholar of some note, having made a translation of Lucretius and written a poem on the Giant's Causeway, the natural phenomenon on the north coast of Ireland. When he had been minister of the second Presbyterian church in Belfast he had run a boarding school.[12] The Strand Street congregation was already Arian when Drummond became second minister in 1815 and when the split came it joined the seceders. John Classon was a prominent member of the congregation.

Ireland had a voluntary association of barristers called the Honourable Society of King's Inns, regulating admission to the profession, but since 1542 Irish law students had been required to spend eight terms (two years) at an English Inn of Court before being called to the Irish bar. The English Inn of Court which Porter joined was not the Temple, as Fanny Classon had proposed, but Gray's Inn, a very popular one with Irishmen in the nineteenth century. He was admitted on 26 May 1827. Subsequently he was admitted a student of the King's Inns, Dublin, in Easter term 1829 and called to the Irish bar in Michaelmas 1831.

While William Porter was keeping his terms in London he lived with his brother John Scott at Rosoman House, Islington Green, where John Scott conducted a school in co-operation with another minister, Rev. David Davison of the Old Jewry. Of his life in London no record has survived except that the two brothers frequently attended debates in the house of commons. They continued to live together sporadically after William had been called to the Irish bar, for William chose to practise on the north-east circuit and John Scott had by this time moved from his London congregation to the first Presbyterian church in Rosemary Street, Belfast and was living at 16 College Square. That and the Classon home in Dublin, 2 Blackhall Place, are the

Portrait of Porter by F. Wolf in the
Houses of Parliament, Cape Town.

Porter in his uniform as captain
of the Cape Volunteer Cavalry.

Hugh Lynar. Porter's lifelong companion.

Below left: The tuition offered by the Artillery Lane School, Londonderry, attended by Porter.

Below right : John Classon. Porter's benefactor, the brother of his stepmother.

EDUCATION.

Artillery-lane School.

THE Rev. W. MOORE, with able Assistants, instructs young Gentlemen in the following branches, viz :—

English,	Projection of Maps,
Writing,	Latin,
Arithmetic,	Greek,
Bookkeeping,	Mathematics, including
History,	Trigonometry, Navigation,
Use of the Globe,	Surveying, Algebra, &c.
Geography,	

The Situation is healthful and commodious. Unremitting attention is paid to the moral and intellectual improvement of the Pupils, and every indulgence is allowed consistent with a strict regard to regularity and application to study.

Terms—6 Guineas per Annum for the Classical Commercial, or Mathematical Branches. 4 Guineas per Annum for Writing and Reading.

Entrance one Guinea.

Vacation one month in Summer—three weeks in Winter.

N. B A few Boarders can be accommodated on moderate terms.

. School will open on Monday 14th August next.

☞ At an Evening School, instructions may be had in Arithmetic, French, and Mathematics. Apply to Mr. PHILSON.

2 Blackhall Place, Dublin. John Classon's residence and Porter's home from the age of 12 till he left Ireland in 1839. This photograph was taken in August 1991.

Northumberland Hotel, Eden Quay, Dublin. One of John Classon's business enterprises. In 1913 the Northumberland Hotel became Liberty Hall, the head-quarters of the Irish Transport and General Workers Union. It was shelled during the Easter Rising of 1916.

COMMERCIAL & FAMILY HOTEL   THE NORTHUMBERLAND   COMMERCIAL & FAMILY HOTEL

King's Inns, Dublin as it was when Porter was called to the bar.

The Four Courts, Dublin in the 1830s.

addresses given for Porter in the list of barristers in the Belfast directory of the 1830s.

The Irish bar was seriously overcrowded in the 1830s. A couple of years after Porter was called, a writer in the *Dublin University Magazine* claimed that the Four Courts were crowded with unemployed barristers. Barristers sometimes waited for years for a brief and many dreaded the circuit because of the unavoidable expense and uncertain return. Barely one in ten succeeded in making a living.[13] Porter himself made another point about the Irish bar; business was not great enough to allow specialisation. Barristers in Ireland, especially juniors, had to take what work came their way, common law, equity, conveyancing, special pleading. To be a pre-eminent success in this general sort of practice demanded great industry and capacity.[14] Porter may have fared better than some of his contemporaries, for his family was well known in the north. In the single surviving letter dating from this period he wrote from Omagh where he had been attending the summer assizes, a friend having got a brief for him in Monaghan. The case turned out disappointingly; the defendant called no witnesses and they were defeated. Porter had no chance to make a speech. Omagh was, of course, his father's home country and he stayed with Robert Walker, the son of his father's half-sister. He confessed himself to be overwhelmed by the number of his relatives in the area, some of whom he had never seen.[15]

Porter was not so fully occupied professionally as not to have time to involve himself in the religious controversy which was of such absorbing interest to northern Protestants at the time, and in which his family was so deeply immersed. When his brother John Scott Porter held a public discussion with Rev. Daniel Bagot of the Church of Ireland on the Unitarian controversy in April 1834 it lasted for four days and was attended by large numbers who paid 4 shillings each for admission.[16] The report of the discussion which was subsequently published ran into four editions. So pleased was his congregation with Porter's performance that they presented him with £1,000.[17] William's contribution to the controversy was to act as secretary of the Irish Unitarian Christian Society, formed in 1830 to spread Unitarian doctrine.[18] He also contributed a series of articles in 1834-35 to the *Bible Christian*, a journal edited by his brother John Scott and founded by the New Light party to counter the message of the *Orthodox Presbyterian*. The articles were on 'Preaching and preachers' and they were a commentary on contemporary evangelical preaching, with an assessment of Rev. Edward Irving, the London evangelical preacher who founded the Holy Catholic Apostolic Church or Irvingites. Starting from the thesis that 'a revolution has taken place in English preaching in great degree analagous to that which has taken place in English poetry,' he went on to inquire into the nature of evangelical preaching, the reasons for its popularity, the kind of religious character which it tended to form, the peculiar nature of the morality it inculcated and its tendency to corrupt. In restrained but uncompromising language he exposed the aspects of evangelicalism to which he objected, its tendency to narrow the intellectual range and impair the mental powers, the contempt it showed for literature and science, its indifference to the splendours of nature, its disregard of human achievements. He poked fun at the excesses of its exponents; he pictured Rev. Edward Irving confronting Daniel O'Connell with a claymore in the great battle he foretold between the armies of the church militant and the combined forces of popery and infidelity; he recorded advertisements in evangelical journals such as 'Two friends of the Lord Jesus wish to borrow £500', and 'Wanted by a steady man a situation as footman in a pious family. His object is to obtain a place where he may live in all honesty and Godly sincerity waiting for the revelation of our Lord Jesus Christ' and he cited an evangelical nobleman who sank a splendid edition of Shakespeare in his pond. He concluded with the reflection that 'their moral purity might not prove permanent and that their excellencies do not exempt them from the common imperfections of humanity'.[19]

Porter did not meddle in Irish politics[20] but, true to his New Light principles, he was a liberal in his political opinions, taking the line on the main issues of the day that was promulgated in his brother-in-law's paper, the *Northern Whig*. Sectarian strife and party spirit he deplored as 'the bane and curse of Ireland'. He welcomed the discomfiture of the landlords during the emancipation crisis when the voters 'whom they had bred like cattle in order to rule like cattle' defied them. One of the things he admired most about O'Connell was his consistent advocacy of negro emancipation in spite of pressure from his American sympathisers. His only regret about Catholic emancipation was that it did not come sooner; he was convinced that what would have been received as a favour if graciously granted in 1825 was 'arrogantly seized as a spoil when wrung from a reluctant ministry in 1829'. Years afterwards, when the Cape franchise was under discussion, he was to draw on this experience to argue powerfully for political generosity. He saw another lost opportunity in the failure of Lord Grey's government to cultivate O'Connell by offering him a judgeship, or even a senior counselship, as Lord Melbourne's government five or six years later was ready to make him master of the rolls, because at the earlier date there were fewer difficulties in the way and he might have accepted and 'left the country in tranquillity'.

Just as Porter was a northern Irish whig on the question of sectarianism, parliamentary reform, slavery and Catholic emancipation, so was he also on the issue of the union of Great Britain and Ireland. He regarded the Act of Union of 1800 as a good measure, though he disapproved of the means by which it had been carried. With O'Connell's mission to effect its repeal he had no sympathy whatsoever.[21] Yet he recognised the stature of the man and the magnitude of his services to his fellow countrymen, for Porter's support of the political union with Britain in no way diminished his attachment to Ireland or his sympathetic understanding of the historical experiences of the Catholic Irish. In the mid-seventeenth century, he believed, they had been the victims of a bloody policy of extermination when they had been 'Cromwell's Kafirs — irreclaimable savages — not to be trusted or tolerated, but to be hunted down like wolves or foxes'. To that had succeeded the wasting policy of the eighteenth-century penal laws which in turn had given place to the irritating policy of disqualification from seats in parliament and a few high offices of state. O'Connell's great achievement was to rid them of their last shackles. When O'Connell died in 1847 Porter recalled the last occasion on which he had seen him address a great meeting of supporters. He remembered the tall, powerfully built figure, the healthy colour in the cheeks, the clear and sonorous voice, the mouth about which there was 'something that strikes you as crafty and unsafe', the confident assurance that since the O'Connells only began to fail at ninety he hoped to live to see repeal.

> We are half amused and half angry at the bold, confident, businesslike way in which such rhapsodies are uttered, but remembering that, with all his faults, he has given Ireland a standing and importance which she did not previously possess. We are vain of the great Irishman and wish him cordially that length of days which he anticipates and which his stalwart frame and buoyant spirits appear to every eye to promise.[22]

1   A grandfather clock was presented to Porter 'by the Newtown Limavady Volunteers in appreciation of a spirited sermon he preached on 20 February 1805'.

2   C. Porter, *Irish Presbyterian biographical sketches*, p.30; R. B. McDowell, *Public opinion and government policy in Ireland*, 1801-1841 pp.38-9.

3   Porter to Mary Eliza Porter, 5 November 1875, SAL, Porter papers; Notes towards a life of his father by Classon Porter. In possession of Rev. Michael Classon.

4   *Second report of commission of Irish Education Inquiry*, H.C. 1826-27, xii (12), 1, pp.430-1.

5   C. Porter, op cit., pp.24-7.

6   G. Brocker, *Rural disorder and police reform in Ireland, 1812-36*, p.167.

7   J. M. Barkley 'The Presbyterian minister in eighteenth-century

Ireland', in *Challenge and conflict*, p.65.

8   Arians denied that Christ was consubstantial with God; Unitarians denied the doctrine of the Trinity and the divinity of Christ.

9   *NW*, 29 January 1829.

10 The synod to which Strand Street Presbyterian church, John Classon's church, was attached.

11 Frances Classon to Rev. William Porter, 15 March 1826. Letter lent to me by the late Aiken McClelland, Ulster Folk and Transport Museum.

12 C. A. Read, *The cabinet of Irish literature*, iii. 165-6; C. H. Irwin, *History of Presbyterianism in Dublin and the south and west of Ireland*, pp.323-4.

13 *Dublin University Magazine*, 1833, i. 45-9.

14 [W. Porter], 'O'Connell', in *Cape of Good Hope Literary Magazine*, no. 3, October 1847, p.272.

15 Porter to Hugh Lynar, 6 August 1836, SAL, Porter papers.

16 *NW*, 17 April 1834.

17 A. Deane (ed), *Belfast Natural History and Philosophical Society centenary volume, 1821-1921*, p.98.

18 C. H. Irwin, op. cit., p.327.

19 Laicus, 'Preaching and preachers', in *Bible Christian*, v. 99-107, 147-56, 229-38, 350-61, 414-24, 464-75, 557-71, vi. 97-111, 309-14, 348-63.

20 *GTJ*, 10 April 1852.

21 He described himself as an outspoken and uncompromising opponent of repeal and he was still 'no friend to what is called Home Rule for Ireland' in 1872. GTJ, 10 April 1852; *Report on Federation G. 9-72* p.80.

22 [W. Porter] 'O'Connell', in op. cit., pp.243-79.

3
Appointment To The Cape Of Good Hope

Porter's appointment was a result of the liberal wind which blew over government and politics in Ireland in the aftermath of the tory collapse of 1830. The accession of the whigs to power was hailed with jubilation by Irish liberals who wholeheartedly endorsed the reform programme. When the house of lords rejected the reform bill in 1831 the *Northern Whig* appeared with black borders in mourning, and when the bill was eventually passed bonfires blazed on the hills above the village of Dunmurry, where Rev. Henry Montgomery had his church. But neither the Irish liberals nor the Catholics who had won emancipation in 1829 reaped any immediate benefit. The new prime minister, Lord Grey, and his colleagues were well-intentioned towards Ireland but the application of liberal principles in a country so riven by bitterness and violence was a daunting task. Various proposals were put forward, including a suggestion by Lord Holland, chancellor of the Duchy of Lancaster, that the dispersal of some legal patronage in the colonies among Irish barristers, especially Catholics, might help the government to counter O'Connell's demand for the repeal of the union. It was not, however, until O'Connell made an informal pact with the whigs to suspend the repeal campaign in return for measures which would give Ireland 'perfect equality of rights, laws and liberties', that a new whig government under Lord Melbourne became committed to a programme of legislative reforms and administrative changes in Ireland. Under the new dispensation O'Connell and influential Irish liberals and Irish whig M.P.s replaced the landed magnates as the effective intermediaries between the office-seeker and the government. When this happened Porter was advantageously placed: as a member of the north-east circuit he was the professional colleague and friend of a number of prominent barristers whose influence was able to secure for him the appointment at the Cape.

The Irish circuits were regularised after the Williamite revolution of 1688-91 when the number was fixed at five: Munster, Leinster, Connaught, the north-west and the north-east, the assize towns in the north-east being Dundalk, Downpatrick, Carrickfergus (later changed to Belfast), Armagh, Monaghan and Drogheda. But even before this, there was a north-east circuit, with a bar society of its own. This society had its records, its property and its officials, and members were ballotted for and formally admitted. Porter became a member in 1832, along with seven others, seven or eight being the normal number of new members to be admitted annually at this time. In Porter's day the society met twice a year, at about six o'clock in the evening in a hotel in or near Dublin, and the formal proceedings were followed by a dinner. It became customary to invite some of the judges or court officials to these dinners. In addition, the bar dined every night in every town on the circuit while the assizes lasted, except in Belfast where only four dinners were held whatever the duration of the assizes. It follows that the members were well known to one another.

One of the outstanding members of the north-east bar society was the man who for many years filled the office of father of the society. Until 1836 the father was the senior member present at a meeting when it opened, but on 30 January 1836 Robert Holmes was appointed permanent father, an office which he held until he left the circuit in 1855. Holmes was very much an anti-establishment figure. He was called to the bar in 1795. At the time of the 1798 rebellion he joined the lawyers' corps of volunteers but resigned after seeing a man being flogged. Another member of the north-east circuit, Henry Joy, thereupon had a resolution passed that only members of the lawyers' corps were worthy of being members of the north-east bar. Holmes challenged Joy to a duel but was arrested and sentenced to six months' imprisonment, three months of which he served. His first wife was a sister of Robert Emmet and after Emmet's rebellion he was again arrested in 1804 but he was released without being put on trial. Though for years he had the largest practice on the north-east circuit he never accepted office or took silk, saying he preferred his stuff gown to all the silk in Macclesfield, the reason reputedly being that he would accept no compliment from Lord Chancellor Plunket who had been one of the prosecuting counsel at Robert Emmet's trial. His final address as defence counsel for the Young Irelander John Mitchel[1] in 1848 was described by the judge as a 'signal and eloquent address — an address that has never been surpassed in a court of justice'.[2] Holmes was one of Porter's backers for the Cape appointment.

Two other members of the north-east circuit whose support Porter enjoyed were Louis Perrin and Mazière Brady, both strong liberals whose abilities went unrecognised until the whigs came to office. Perrin became a justice of the king's bench in 1832 and Brady attorney general of Ireland in 1838, chief baron of the exchequer in 1840 and lord chancellor in 1841. It was Brady who told Porter of his appointment. These two, like Holmes, were Protestants, but Porter was also recommended for the Cape appointment by David Richard Pigot, one of the Catholic liberal barristers who also first attained office under the whigs, becoming solicitor general in 1839, attorney general in 1840 and chief baron in 1846. The man who was in the best position to further Porter's interests was another of his seniors in the north-east bar society, William Curry, a member since 1806, a bencher of the Honourable Society of King's Inns in Dublin and third sergeant-at-law. Curry was whig M.P. for Armagh in 1838 when a report appeared in the *Northern Whig* that Anthony Oliphant, attorney general of the Cape Colony, had been raised to the bench as chief justice of Ceylon. It was on Curry's application, endorsed by Porter's other influential friends in the north-east bar society, that he was appointed to succeed Oliphant.[3]

He was not the first choice for the office. At the beginning of February 1839 the appointment of Patrick Matthias Murphy was announced. Murphy, who had been active in anti-repeal circles, was dissatisfied with the terms of the appointment and withdrew. The office was then offered to Joseph Nelson, a friend of Porter and a fellow member of the north-east bar society; he had been called to the Irish bar the year before Porter. He too declined and on 19 March 1839 Porter's appointment was announced in the *London Gazette*.[4] The post carried a salary of £1,200 a year, with permission to practise at the Cape bar in cases in which the crown was not involved.

The appointment of a man with Porter's opinions and background to so lucrative a post would have been unthinkable a few years before when the tory gentry held sway in Ireland. In the new climate created by the O'Connell-whig accord reform began to take root. Between 1835 and 1840 several measures were passed — a tithe act, a poor-law act and a municipal corporation act — but the government's tardiness in pushing them through, and their limited scope, convinced O'Connell that the union could never work to Ireland's advantage. Even before the whigs fell from power his thoughts were turning again to repeal.

More impressive than the whig government's legislative record were the changes it effected in the character of the Irish administration. Under the guidance of the under-secretary, Thomas Drummond, an attempt was made to inspire confidence in the impartiality of the administration and so present the Irish government in a more favourable light to Irish Catholics. Drummond continued the practice, begun by the tories, of appointing stipendiary magistrates under the control of the Irish government to replace unpaid magistrates who were known for their class or anti-Catholic bias. Catholics were encouraged to enlist in the reorganised police force, and the army was no longer employed in the collection of tithes or the eviction of tenants. Drummond did not share the landlords' belief in the efficacy of coercive legislation. When the magistrates of Tipperary demanded strong measures after a landlord in the county had been murdered in 1838 he created a furore by replying that property had its duties as well as its rights and that the disturbed state of the country stemmed from the neglect of those duties in the past.[5] He also acted vigorously against the Orange Order. Orange demonstrations were prohibited, other activities were restricted and magistrates with Orange sympathies were dismissed.

Even more striking evidence of the new spirit abroad was the policy adopted in the filling of public offices. Catholic lawyers were appointed to high legal posts, one of them, Michael O'Loghlen, being raised to the bench as a baron of the exchequer in 1836, the first Catholic judge to be appointed in Ireland since the reign of James II. O'Connell himself was offered the mastership of the rolls. Three of the six Irish judges appointed between 1835 and 1840 were Catholics, all of them were liberals and four had been whig M.P.s. During this time, either the attorney general or the solicitor general was a Catholic. Liberal Protestants who had no aristocratic connections also received more generous treatment than before. O'Connell was well pleased with the way the policy was shaping in the spring of 1839. 'They have freed us' he declared, 'from Orange domination and persecution; they have muzzled the ferocious tiger and drawn the fangs from the persecuting wolves'.[6] In the circumstances of the time it was possible for a man with Porter's New Light views to obtain a public appointment.

Unlike some of the whig government's appointments, the selection of Porter won general approval. The *Northern Whig* was naturally gratified, and the *Newry Examiner*, described as a paper of the extreme left, declared that it could not have spoken less warmly of so excellent a person without doing wrong to genius and virtue 'such as we can seldom hope to meet on the highways of the world'. But equally, the conservative and Orange *Ulster Times* expressed its respect for Porter's professional and personal character and its satisfaction at hearing of his advancement even though he was a political opponent. At a personal level, too, Porter's appointment was celebrated. In his home town of Limavady a dinner in his honour was held on 6 May 1839 in the Queen's Arms Hotel, attended by his father, his brothers and his friend Hugh Lynar. Among the fifty or so guests were representatives of every political party and every religious denomination. Local gentry from as far as forty kilometres away were there, the land agents of the great landlords in the area, local merchants, doctors and clergymen, both Presbyterian and Church of Ireland, including Rev. George Vaughan Sampson, a former headmaster of Foyle College, Londonderry and author of the *Statistical survey of the county of Londonderry*. An apology for absence was received from the local parish priest, Rev. Edward O'Hagan.[7] A week later another dinner was held for him in the Salthill Hotel on the outskirts of Dublin. This time all those present, upwards of seventy, were members of the Irish bar. At the end of his career Porter referred to the occasion as one of the three great compliments he had received in his lifetime; the tribute of such men, many of them eminent, to an obscure figure like himself had moved him profoundly, he said. He recalled telling them that although he could never hope to repay the debt every man owed his profession by the display of great abilities or great attainments he hoped, with his 'heart-fixed hatred of injustice' so to conduct himself in the distant colony that the honour of the bar of Ireland would not suffer at his hands.[8]

Taking leave of his family was more painful. On the day before he left Ireland he said good-bye to his elderly and ailing benefactress Frances Classon and the last thing he did before his ship moved down the Thames was to write to her, as he had promised to do. An obligation to his father to keep a journal during his journey he also discharged. A few hours before setting off he wrote a short note to each of his brothers and to his sister, 'to show that I remember you'. The letter to Classon concluded, 'Farewell. The record of old times is written in my heart and can never be obliterated. Farewell'.[9] When the moment of departure came he was filled with sadness. As the packet-boat put out from Kingstown (Dunlaoghaire) he watched his friends on the jetty and the familiar landmarks recede into the distance until 'the land where live the living and lie the dead who loved me as I shall not again be loved was hidden from my sight and the cloud that descended upon it settled cold upon my heart'.[10]

Yet Porter was anxious to take up his duties at the Cape as soon as possible. Even before his appointment was officially announced he went to London to make preparations for his departure and from there he wrote to the colonial secretary, the marquis of Normanby, telling him that he hoped to be ready by the first week in May.[11]

By mid-May, however, he had still not been able to find transport, though business and other friends were constantly on the watch for a suitable vessel sailing from either London or Liverpool. The problem was that the Indiamen could not be induced to touch at the Cape at this time of year and that any Cape traders which had been available were invariably small and wretchedly equipped. Porter had heard that colonial officials were sometimes transported in a naval vessel, but he did not press any claim. Subsequently he was told that it would be contrary to custom to order a passage for him on a naval ship but if one was going to the Cape he could approach the officer in command.[12] A few days later, however, he learnt of a trader called the *Sterling* which was due to sail the following month. She was small and had limited accommodation but if nothing better was available he proposed to take passage on her. That these practical arrangements were combined with efforts to brief himself for his new career is shown by his request to the colonial office to be shown an unpublished report made by the commissioners appointed to inquire into the administration of the law at the Cape. James Stephen, the under-secretary, raised no objections but he pointed out that the Cape judges, the Cape attorney general, Oliphant, and he himself had been unable to understand it and that was why it had never been published.[13]

When Porter set out for the Cape he was accompanied by his friend Hugh Lynar, who was to remain a life-long companion. They had met soon after Porter's arrival in Dublin at the age of twelve, when Lynar was fourteen. Very little is known about Lynar's background. He had a brother who died in 1836, but apart from that there is no information about his family. When he died at the Cape many years later his death certificate was filled in by Porter. Under the heading 'Parents' he wrote, 'Forgotten, if ever known'. Lynar was originally trained as a printer and eventually had premises in the Northumberland Buildings on Eden Quay, Dublin. Later he managed to improve his education; he was studying Latin in 1836.[14] When he was leaving Dublin in 1839 a group of his friends in the printing business presented him with an address congratulating him on having elevated himself 'to a station above that in which you originally started'.[15] They were referring to the fact that he was editor of the *Morning Register*, a liberal daily which supported whig reforms in Ireland. Charles Gavan Duffy, the Young Irelander and subsequently prime minister of Victoria, who worked as a subeditor on the *Register* in Lynar's time, described him as

a Unitarian from Ulster ... a man of integrity and capacity who probably found the task of conducting a journal essentially Catholic rendered tolerable by the opportunity it afforded of supporting the policy of the Mulgrave administration ... which an enlightened whig like Lynar could unreservedly applaud.[16] Whatever his origins, Lynar was highly thought of by both the Classon and Porter families. The building in which he had his printing and stationery business was owned by John Classon; Fanny Classon told Porter on the eve of his departure, 'In Hugh you have the best substitute this world could afford for all you have left behind'; and Porter's father began a letter to Lynar at the Cape with the words, 'My dearest Hugh, with truth may I use the expression, for there is not another Hugh in existence half so dear to me as you are'.[17]

1   Mitchel was on board the convict ship *Neptune* whose arrival
     precipitated the anti-convict crisis at the Cape.
2   G. H. Smith, *The north-east bar*, pp.15-20, 31-2, 61; J. R. O'Flanagan, *The
     Irish bar*, pp.274-80.
3   *NW*, 3 November 1839, 23 February 1839; Dod, *Parliamentary
     companion*, 1838, pp.49, 98; 'Note book of an Irish barrister', in
     Metropolitan Magazine, xxxvii (1843); J. S. Porter to Lord Palmerston,
     PRO, CO 48/371/457.
4   NW, 23 February 1839; *London Gazette*, 4 February 1839, 19 March 1839;
     SACA, 10 July 1839.
5   The letter, sent in Drummond's name, is said to have been written by
     the Irish attorney general, Stephen Woulfe, one of the first Catholic
     barristers to obtain preferment. J. R. O'Flanagan, *The Irish bar* (London,
     1879), p.262.
6   *NW*, 25 May 1839.
7   Ibid., 23 March, 11 May, 25 May 1839.
8   *Freeman's Journal*, 17 May 1839; *GTJ*, 28 August 1865.
9   Porter to Classon Porter, 17 June 1839. Letter in the possession of Mr
     Basil Porter, Port Elizabeth, Classon's great-grandson.
10   Journal, SAL, Porter papers. This account of his experiences from 16
     September to 16 November 1839 was written in fulfilment of a promise
     to his father.
11   Porter to Normanby, 16 March 1839; PRO CO 48/206/193.
12   Same to same, 16 May 1839, ibid., f.204.
13   Same to same, ibid., ff.208, 210-11.
14   Porter to Lynar, 6 August 1836, SAL, Porter papers.
15   Address to Hugh Lynar, esq., (n.d.), ibid.
16   GTJ, 28 July 1873; S. J. Brown, *The press in Ireland*, p.26; B. Inglis, *The
     freedom of the press in Ireland, 1784-1841*, p.218; C. Gavan Duffy, *My life
     in two hemispheres*, i.35.
17   Rev. William Porter to Lynar, 10 March 1841, SAL, Porter papers.

4

Passage To Cape Town

Porter left Ireland on the first stage of his journey to the Cape on the evening of Monday 17 June 1839. He was accompanied by Hugh Lynar. After a crossing smooth enough not to upset even so bad a sailor as Porter, the vessel reached Liverpool at six o'clock the next morning and he and Lynar travelled by train to London, where they stayed with an old friend, Joseph Chamberlain, at 36 Milk Street, Cheapside. Porter was busy in London. Sitting for a drawing for his uncle took up a good deal of time because Eddis,[1] the artist, lived away in Newman Street, off Oxford Street; so too did laying in provisions for the voyage: preserved meats and soups which, in the outcome, they never had occasion to use, arrowroot which stood Porter in good stead on board, and soda powders which Lynar was glad to have. He also paid a visit to Justice Perrin, who was staying at Putney Park, to thank him for his part in securing the Cape appointment. The queen held a levee during his stay and he was advised to go to it. He did not take the occasion too seriously. He hired a court dress which he said fitted tolerably, though a little too short at the knees and the coat a little too short at the back — he was six feet two inches tall — procured a coach with a driver and footman 'of a most imposing respectability' and set off for St James'. He was to be presented by the marquis of Normanby, a mere humbug, as he said, for his lordship was not present at the levee but had given permission through a third party for his name to be used. There was a considerable crowd of people, mostly in uniform, but only three known to Porter: O'Loghlen, the Irish master of the rolls, Pigot, the Irish solicitor general and a police magistrate called Kelly. From Pigot he got some hints on how to behave, particularly not to kneel too close to the queen, for that might seem wanting in respect, nor so far off that the queen would have to stretch over to him. As he proceeded through the apartments reflecting on 'the proper manner of performing my Ko To' he encountered an ecclesiastical dignitary even more perplexed than himself so he passed on the advice he had been given and was warmly thanked. Eventually he reached the reception chamber. The presentations were done so quickly that he had no more than a momentary view of the queen. What with her dress and the excitement of the occasion he was more impressed than he had expected. She was a mere girl but decidedly a good looking one, he thought. There was a dash of decision in the expression of her face which relieved it of feebleness and her figure, though petite, was not bad. Then his card was presented 'and the queen heard, and heard, I must say with astonishing indifference, that Her Attorney General at the Cape was now before her'. When told to kneel he misjudged his position and found himself with his nose almost in contact with the queen's wrist. In desperation he dipped his chin, protruded his lips as much as possible and contrived to kiss her hand.

Porter was a great admirer of Macaulay, as much for his literary style and oratory as for his political views. He went to the house of commons in the hope, if not of hearing him speak, at least of seeing him. But Macaulay was not in the house that night. So he decided to send him a note requesting an interview. When he received an off-putting reply he was considerably annoyed. The speeches he heard in the commons did not impress him greatly; though his friend Edward Litton was more fluent than he had anticipated, Creswell of Liverpool fell far short of his expectations; Morgan John O'Connell, he thought, did better in the Law Debating Society in Dublin and as for Lord John Russell, 'Lord Johnny', 'while he was saying his say we found we could stand the thing no longer and came away'. He was disappointed, too, by the performance of the two leading ladies in the opera he attended.

The ship on which he was to sail, the *Sterling,* a barque of 360 tons, lay in St Catherine's Dock. He and Lynar took one of the large stern cabins and a smaller one opening off it, paying for both £115. They went on board with their friends to try out the cot or hammock Porter had been recommended to buy but when he climbed into it and was given a rocking by his cousin he was within an ace of being seasick.

After breakfast on 28 June, Porter and his friends went to London Bridge to catch the nine o'clock steamer to Gravesend, the *Sterling* having hauled out of dock and dropped down to Gravesend the evening before to take on stores. It was a cold and drizzling day and the dreariness of their surroundings fitted their depressed spirits. At Gravesend, a ship anchored in the middle of the river, green with cabbages and turnips hanging everywhere about her lower riggings, proved to be the *Sterling.* Taking one of the many small boats plying for hire they pushed off for their temporary home. In the cabin Porter wrote several letters, the last, according to promise, to Aunt Fanny. Then the time came to say farewell to the two friends who had come on board with him; they went ashore on the boat that had brought them over and Porter and Lynar were left alone. 'That was the loneliness'. At three o'clock the *Sterling* got under way and was towed by a steam boat to the Downs where she cast anchor for the night. Porter, not relishing the idea of getting into his cot, slept on a five foot sofa, 'to the no small annoyance of my legs'.

Now he had leisure to observe the crew and his fellow passengers. He thought highly of the captain, Gabriel Forster. He had risen from the ranks, was active and intelligent, a good seaman and a good man. He did his duty by the passengers well and deserved the respect they had for him. He had picked up a smattering of many things but was particularly interested in literature and medicine. He was an enthusiastic, though execrable, reader and read to everybody who would listen to him. Yet for a man who had a book so often in his hands 'his expressions were far from being always scrupulously classical'; he was given to assenting a great deal in conversation and the words he invariably used were 'exactically so'. When Porter asked about a sick passenger for whom he had prescribed he replied 'Better, a good deal, although her pulse is still extremely flatulent'. The other officers were less admirable; Ford, the first mate, was a drunkard and the second mate was incompetent. There were only five adult passengers, in addition to Lynar and Porter: Hanna, a young Irish barrister, Townshend, a London business-man accompanied by his nephew, Syme, a medical student returning to Cape Town, a lad called Stanbridge going to join his brother in business at the Cape, Mrs Gubb, the wife of a cap-tain who traded between the Cape and Calcutta, and a steerage passenger called Smith, a baker with six children, three sons and three daughters. All were eminently respectable. Porter listened sympathetically to Smith's account of his hard life and resolved to befriend him if he could. He christened the Londoner Mr Pickwick because of his appearance.

They had an easy passage down the Channel and in a few days lost sight of land. Up to this point Porter was tolerably well, apart from slight nausea, but when they entered the Bay of Biscay he suffered agonies of seasickness for several days and nights. Heavy doses of calomel in the evening and of castor oil in the morning brought no improvement. Eventually a bottle of ale, boiling hot and thickened with ground ginger, gave him some relief but what he longed for most in his misery was a bunch of grapes. Food was out of the question during this time but when his sickness abated somewhat he found the ship abun-dantly provided with essentials. The ship's boat was laid up on deck and divided into two sections in one of which were a dozen well-fed pigs and in the other half a dozen sheep in fine condition. Numerous hencoops were ranged round the vessel filled with geese, ducks and fowl. The fowl proved to be as tough as leather, the mutton good and the pork splendid. What they missed most was fresh bread and milk. The loaves brought from London were soon eaten, attempts to bake on board failed, and they were reduced to eating biscuit. Milk was an even greater problem. They had what was described as preserved milk but Porter thought it more like 'indifferent drawn butter'. He and Lynar found it so nauseating in their tea and coffee that they gave up drinking either. For breakfast they had brandy and water or sometimes a bottle of claret with cold pork and boiled rice. Lunch was at 12.30 and Porter usually had something like a slice of salt beef and a glass of ale. Dinner was served punctually at 3 o'clock. The Portuguese cook, dirty though he was, made excellent pea soup. They had it four times a week, not half often enough for Porter. But he refused 'to tear away at the cordage of some old skeletons of cocks', preferring instead a helping of delicious pork. The tea, handed round at seven o'clock, Porter shunned like poison. At nine o'clock or thereabouts he had some gin and water before going down to his cabin.

Meals punctuated a monotonous day. Porter woke about seven o'clock in his swinging cot, usually feeling as if he had 'a Saxony salt mine' in the pit of his stomach. With difficulty he scrambled out of the cot on to the oilcloth floor, fortunate if he did not knock his head against the roof of the cabin or tumble, through reaching the floor just as the ship lurched. He then sat down on the sofa and seized his 'unmentionables'. When he had summoned up enough energy he inserted first one leg and then the other. Shaving was a difficult task, for he was apt to be flung across the cabin if the ship suddenly keeled. By this time he was beginning to feel squeamish so he finished dressing hurriedly and scrambled up on deck. There he either lay on a mattress under an awning or, if he felt well enough, sauntered slowly about the vessel looking at the boys feeding the fowl or watching the pigs being washed. Undressing at night was easy enough, but not getting into his cot; he had to stand on the sofa and launch himself in on one side at the risk of rolling out at the other. When conditions improved other activities became possible, though throughout the voyage Porter found it impossible to write and difficult to read. Still, by taking advantage of every quiet moment he managed to get through Justinian's *Institutes*, Van der Linden's *Koopman's handboek*, Browne's *Civil law*, and Hallifax's *Analysis of Roman civil law* three or four times and to read de Beaumont's *L'Irlande*, Mme de Stael's novel *Corinne*, a volume of the Baptist divine Robert Hall's *Sermons* and Sir Thomas Brown's *Religio Medici* and *Hydriotaphia*.

An old fiddle belonging to the steward's assistant provided the music for an hour or two's dancing before bedtime. They could muster only two ladies, Mrs Gubb and Smith the baker's eldest daughter, but sometimes Captain Forster and sometimes Porter himself 'figured as a fair one'. At this stage of the voyage the first mate, Ford, took to entertaining the passengers, and horrifying some of them, by spinning yarns about pirates he had known in these waters. The more blood-curdling the story the funnier he seemed to find it and Porter suspected that he was laughing at their supposed gullibility. He concluded that Ford was a liar of the first magnitude. Porter derived a lot of pleasure from watching the porpoises playing about the ship and he was sorry when Captain Forster harpooned one. When it had been hauled on deck a considerable quantity of oil was extracted from the carcase and the flesh was eaten by the sailors for dinner next day. As they approached the equator great schools of flying fish appeared and now and then some of the dolphins that pursued them. Sometimes in the morning they found a flying fish on deck and used it as bait to fish for dolphins but the only dolphin taken was one that was harpooned. There was much stir when a shark was spotted swimming astern. With a large piece of pork as bait a line was thrown out and after an exciting time the shark was hooked and brought aboard.

They had expected intense heat at the equator and consequently were agreeably surprised to find that the temperature in the cabin never rose above 85°F and that the heat on deck was by no means overpowering. On this part of the voyage the captain, 'Mr Pickwick', young Stanbridge, Lynar and Porter used to come on deck every morning in their drawers to get a shower from the leather tube attached to the pump which brought up the water to wash the decks. On the evening of the day before they crossed the line they had their first intimation of the horse-play associated with that event. Porter was pacing the deck, enjoying the stillness of the night, when he heard the voice of Neptune hail the ship and proclaiming his intention of coming aboard next day at eleven o'clock — the voice was suspiciously like that of George, a large, rough, rollicking sailor. All was bus-tle next morning. The pigs and sheep were dispossessed and the none-too-clean boat was filled with black bilge. At the appoin-ted time the passengers were summoned on deck to find an oddly attired group representing Neptune and his attendants. Lynar, on behalf of the passengers, offered tribute and they were hailed as real gentlemen but the sailors who were crossing the line for the first time were subjected to rough treatment, cul-minating in a dousing in the boat.

Once well south of the equator they began to feel that the worst of the journey was over. At this time it became clear that the first mate was seldom sober. He was perpetually swearing at the men, threatening to brain one of them with a handspike and telling another that he would cut his liver out. Then one day when the breeze was blowing moderately the ship began to roll in a very peculiar way and on looking up they saw the sails fluttering loosely. In an instant the captain rushed on deck, found the mate drunk at the helm and the ship quite out of her course. He took remedial action at once. Had the weather been bad the consequences might have been serious but they escaped with the loss of the maintop mast. For this misconduct, added to his previous lapses, Ford was confined to his cabin for the rest of the voyage and discharged when they reached Cape Town. The episode had a sequel. A report, traced to Ford, was spread about the ship that the captain had behaved improperly with a female passenger, presumably Mrs Gubb. When it reached the captain's ears he immediately asked the gentlemen on board to investigate the charge. At first they were reluctant to do so but they eventually agreed. After a searching inquiry, directed by Porter, they came to the unanimous conclusion that the charge was false, scandalous and malicious.

All this time they were driving southwards. The flying fish grew scarce and finally disappeared. Porter was beginning to long for some distraction when an albatross came in sight. Presently it was joined by several others and for the last three weeks or so of the voyage two or more were always flying round the ship. There were several smaller birds, too, which the sailors called Cape hens [white-chinned petrel] and crowds of a graceful sort of gull, striped zebra-like, known as Cape pigeons. [They are in fact a species of petrel.]

At last on 15 September, Porter's 34th birthday, when they had been seventy-nine days at sea, land was sighted from the masthead. The news gave Porter no pleasure: though he had suffered much at sea and was never really well enough to enjoy himself he was reluctant to disembark and feel himself a stranger in a strange land. Still, he went up to the foretop to have a look for himself and there, sure enough, was land. That evening the passengers were all busy packing. In the morning when they came on deck they were at the mouth of Table Bay and had their first close view of the coast — 'a bold, striking, County Antrim kind of coast' — and of Robben Island lying immediately to their north. When they entered Table Bay the village of Green Point came in sight and they saw horsemen and some carriages on the road. Then when they sailed past the Lion's Rump they had the first full view of Table Mountain and of Cape Town with its flat-roofed, whitewashed houses and its streets running down to the water edge. They cast anchor at nine o'clock, opposite the town about a mile out. In half an hour the deputy port captain and the health officer came on board and when everything was found in order the flag of health was hoisted. Immediately a boat which had been sailing round the ship for some time ran alongside and a man scrambled aboard. His mission was to secure Porter's services for the defence in a pending law-suit. When Porter accepted the case he was handed five guineas 'to refresh my memory'. Disembarkation began at once. The passengers with some of their light luggage were rowed through the heavy surf to the slight wooden pier which projected a little into the bay. At one o'clock Porter set foot in the colony.[2]

1   Eden Upton Eddis (1812-1901) was a portrait artist noted for his pencil portraits. He painted such famous people as Sydney Smith and Lord Macaulay.
2   Based on Journal, SAL, Porter papers.

PART II

The Cape Years

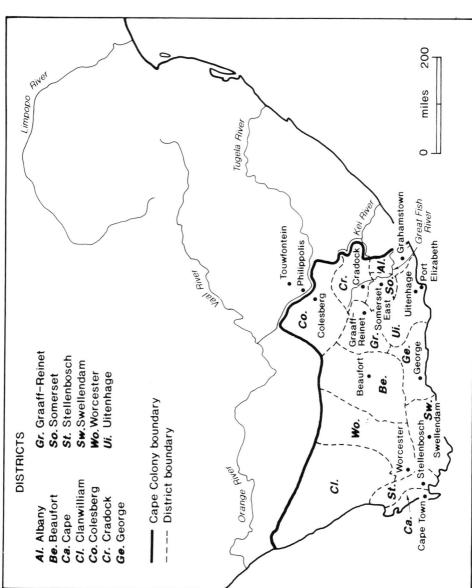

DISTRICTS

Al. Albany   *Gr.* Graaff–Reinet
Be. Beaufort   *So.* Somerset
Ca. Cape   *St.* Stellenbosch
Cl. Clanwilliam   *Sw.* Swellendam
Co. Colesberg   *Wo.* Worcester
Cr. Cradock   *Ui.* Uitenhage
Ge. George

—— Cape Colony boundary
---- District boundary

Cape Colony and Districts, 1820

5
Porter In The Cape Context

The colony in which Porter had arrived to take up his appointment was a recent addition to the British empire. The expedition to occupy the Cape sailed from Cork two weeks before he was born and the colony was ceded by the Dutch only twenty-five years before his arrival. It was still in the process of being anglicised and brought into the mainstream of British imperial development. Porter's office of attorney general had been in existence for just over a decade and other institutions and procedures in which Porter was to be involved had an even shorter history. By the time he left South Africa thirty-four years later the Cape had attained the status of a self-governing colony, its area had expanded and its population increased in numbers and complexity, the place of the coloured population in society had been defined, the variety and volume of its economic activity had grown, and other white states, Natal and the two Boer republics, the Transvaal and the Orange Free State, had come into being. Towards many of these developments Porter made a notable contribution and his principles and ideas did much to shape the mould in which they were cast.

Porter joined a society at the Cape even more complex and problem-ridden than the one he had left in Ireland. The white colonists who pre-dated the British were an amalgam of Dutch, Germans and French Huguenots. Although considerable differences in outlook and way of life had developed between the settled population of Cape Town and its hinterland and the pastoral farmers or Boers of the interior they were essentially a single community, bound together by family ties, by the Calvinist Dutch Reformed church and by a distinct language, Dutch, or a local variant of it. They were outnumbered by the survivors of the indigenous Khoikhoi and San, then called Hottentots and Bushmen, the ex-slaves, mainly negroes from east and west Africa and Malays from the East Indies, and a mixed race, produced by miscegenation between whites and these coloured peoples. By the time of Porter's arrival a new element had been added. At the end of a frontier war in 1835-36, one of a series of wars spread over a hundred years between the colonists on the eastern frontier and the black peoples beyond it, a group of Fingos or Mfengu from beyond the colony's eastern frontier, was settled within the colony. By this time, too, Xhosa and others from beyond the frontier were being allowed into the colony to search for work, but these 'native foreigners' were not regarded as subjects of the colony. British settlers had been few in the early days of British rule but a government-sponsored emigration scheme in 1820 resulted in some 4,000 people from the British Isles being settled on the eastern frontier.

From that time the colony as Porter found it began to take shape. The judicial system of which he was a part was reorganised by a charter of justice in 1827 which established a supreme court, replaced the fiscal by an attorney general and provided for trial by jury in criminal cases. Between 1823 and 1828 English became the official language of the courts and of government and the criminal law became largely English, though Roman-Dutch civil law continued in use. At local level civil commissioners and resident magistrates replaced the machinery inherited from the Dutch, and provision was made for the setting up of municipal bodies in towns and villages. Judicial and administrative reforms coincided with changes designed to expand civil liberties. Freedom of the press was conceded in 1828. In the same year an ordinance relieved the free coloured people from the need to carry passes and confirmed their right to own land and to be given contracts of service by their employers. But the major development in this field was the British decision to abolish slavery throughout the empire. In 1834 slaves at the Cape were freed, although they had to serve an apprenticeship to their former owners which terminated just about the time of Porter's arrival.

As attorney general Porter was *ex officio* a member of the executive council and of the legislative council. These bodies were also the product of the era of change at the Cape. When the settlement was under British occupation during the French war and for long after its cession in 1814 it was governed as a crown colony, with a governor exercising autocratic rule, subject only to the control of the secretary of state for war and the colonies in London. In 1825 the first step towards diluting the governor's powers was taken with the setting up of an advisory council of nominated officials, to whom two unofficial members were added in 1827. With pressure growing in Cape Town for some form of popular representation the whig government in Britain replaced the council in 1834 by an executive council, consisting of the four principal office holders, and a legislative council made up of the same four officials, the auditor general and from five to seven nominated members. The governor, who presided over both bodies, had to consult his executive council and explain his action to the secretary of state if he rejected its advice and he had to submit financial and other ordinances to the legislative council for approval and justify himself to the imperial government if he vetoed the council's decision.

Many of these innovations, introduced in such rapid succession, gave offence to the conservative frontier Boers. They were dissatisfied, too, with the Cape government's response to black incursions into the colony. Their resentment combined with the lure of unoccupied land beyond the frontier to set in motion a dramatic exodus from the colony. The Great Trek was an organised migration of people in search of a new home beyond the range of British authority. They called themselves emigrants. By mid-1837 about 5,000 of them had crossed the Orange river. The movement was still in progress when Porter reached the Cape and the problems it created were amongst those that were to exercise him.

Porter arrived in the colony at a time when its economy was expanding. The introduction of merino sheep and experiments in crossbreeding with native stock, combined with the demand for raw wool in Britain following on the mechanisation of the wool manufacturing industry, brought prosperity to the sheep farmers and a significant increase in the volume of wool exports. The development of commercial agriculture stimulated the growth of private business. The growth of trade underlined the need for improvements in communications, and major developments in road construction were put in hand by Porter's colleague John Montagu, the colonial secretary, in the 1840s. Further evidence of the growing sophistication of the economy is seen in the appearance of insurance companies from the 1830s and in the founding in Cape Town of the first commercial bank, the Cape of Good Hope Bank, in 1837. This was quickly followed by the opening of the South African Bank, also in Cape Town, in 1838 and the Eastern Province Bank in Grahamstown in 1839. Both Porter and Lynar were to invest profitably in these and other enterprises.

Yet in spite of this spate of activity in so many fields the colony was still something of a backwater at the end of the thirties. The white population was sparse and thinly spread over vast distances, with the result that there were great differences in social patterns and in the response to current problems. The major concentration was in the Cape peninsula and Cape Town, with a population of about 18,000, was the only town of any size in the colony. Elsewhere, such urban centres as existed were small, some of them mere villages. Even in the administrative centres the drostdy, or seat of the magistracy, and the Dutch Reformed church were often the only buildings of any note. Grahamstown, five hundred miles away on the eastern frontier, was the second largest town with a population of about 3,500 in the mid-thirties. In the long-settled west the rural population of wine and grain farmers lived in a manner reflecting their degree of prosperity, which in some cases was considerable. There were prosperous farmers, too, in the more favoured areas elsewhere in the colony. But the pastoralist Boers of the interior led an isolated and self-contained life, linked only to urban centres by their need for the necessities they could not produce themselves, like iron and gunpowder, and by their practice of attending the quarterly nagmaal or communion service of the Dutch Reformed church in the nearest town or village. Their standard of living was unpretentious and their vision limited but their hospitality to travellers was openhanded. On the eastern frontier, in the area occupied by the 1820 settlers, English influences prevailed, but exposure to the dangers of the frontier had bred in them, as in the Boers, a profound distrust of the philanthropic ideas about the indigenous peoples emanating from the west, and a conviction that their interests were ill-served by the authorities in far-off Cape Town.

Cape Town was the hub of the Cape universe, the seat of government, the link with the outside world, the long-established leader in the social and economic life of the colony. When Porter took up residence there it was described as a Dutch-looking town. The principal street, the Heerengracht, was tree-lined, with a canal in the middle crossed by foot-bridges. To the indignation of the residents shops were beginning to appear and a hotel called the George had opened in it. It ran from the Grand Parade to the government gardens, with their oak-lined public walk and government house. The Grand Parade, adjacent to the castle and surrounded by a belt of trees, provided another promenade for the citizens. At the north-east end of the Parade stood the commercial exchange which served as a centre for the business community but also housed the public library and had a hall suitable for public functions. The white, flat-roofed houses had raised stoeps facing the street and gardens irrigated by little streams. In the vicinity of the beach there were some public buildings: the old gaol, with its treadmill, the custom-house and the post office, but also less salubrious areas, the town shambles, the fish market and the worst slums. The high, wooden jetty near the castle was the only harbour facility, though a second jetty, shorter and lower, which Porter went to inspect soon after his arrival, was in course of construction. Beyond the town on the pleasant, wooded slopes of Table Mountain stood the elegant houses and gardens of the Cape Town elite.

Cape Town society was dominated by the prosperous merchants, some of them, like Hamilton Ross, of relatively recent British origin, others, like the van der Byls, belonging to the Dutch-speaking community of older lineage. Such men mixed on terms of equality with the senior colonial officials and with the officers of the garrison who constituted a floating population. Other temporary residents of good social standing were the 'Hindoos' or 'Indians', civilian and military personnel from India who elected to spend their furlough at the Cape instead of returning to Britain partly because the overland route via Egypt — let alone the Suez canal — had not yet been developed and partly because they could still draw their allowances at the Cape. At the other end of the social scale the working class was composed of the ex-slaves and the coloured population. The slaves had just completed their period of apprenticeship and Porter found great dissatisfaction among employers about the dislocation of the labour market and the problems caused by the sudden influx of the slave compensation money. Many of the slaves, especially the Malays, had acquired skills as artisans in the days of slavery and they continued to ply their trades as free men after emancipation. Domestic service absorbed a good many of the coloured people. Others were fishermen, dockers or general labourers. Visitors were struck by the diversity of types, black, yellow, brown and near white, and by the colourful spectacle they presented. Porter's immediate impression on landing was that here was a place where the climate called people out of doors:

> Seats along the fronts of the houses, for the most part occupied; all sorts of merchandise exposed for sale on the Parade; here, a barber shaving a black fellow in the street, there a number of unemployed coolies lying listlessly upon the ground; everything savoured of the south.[1]

Such was the *milieu* in which Porter embarked on his career. That he became so highly esteemed and influential was due in some measure to the accident of circumstances, the fact that he was appointed when the colony was in process of being transformed from a strategic outpost into a normal component of the British empire. Any man in an official position at such a time of transition had it in his power to influence the course of events to an extent commensurate with his ability, his interest and his opportunity. In all of these respects Porter was well fitted for a major role. The success with which he availed himself of the situation was also in part due to the nature of the colony at the time. It was a remote and sparsely populated territory. The number of able men in public life was limited, even within official circles. A man of moderate competence could attain a prominence in such a context far greater than he would have reached in a more populous and sophisticated society. A man of Porter's talents was bound to stand out like a shining light among his contemporaries at the Cape. Another factor which added enormously to the strength of the influence he was able to exert, as time went on, was his protracted tenure of the same office. He held the post of attorney general for twenty-six years, longer than any other office-holder in the colony of his day. Governors were birds of passage, colonial secretaries in Britain came and went: seven governors and fifteen colonial secretaries held office while he was attorney general. By the very length of his service Porter became the accepted authority on Cape affairs.

Porter's reputation, however, did not rest on chance circumstances alone. He had personal and intellectual qualities which inspired confidence and respect. He was an impressive figure, six feet two inches tall, handsome, with a dignified bearing and a melodious voice. His oratorical skill and his flair for lucid exposition made him a formidable protagonist. His familiarity with English literature, his wit and sense of humour, his fund of anecdotes, his eye for detail and his awareness of his surroundings all contributed to the enrichment of his conversation. His humanity and generosity, his skill in public speaking and his social graces made him an acceptable figure in Cape society and a leader in charitable activities. In short, he was one of the best-known and most popular men in the Cape Town of his day.

Popularity and ability would not, of course, in themselves have constituted an adequate basis for an influential role in public life. It was the office Porter held, and the duties which went with it, that opened up the avenues to power and made him so significant a figure in the history of Cape liberalism. There were other liberals at the Cape in his day, men like Saul Solomon who carried his liberalism, as Porter's brother-in-law Frank Dalzell Finlay did, to the naming of his children — William Ewart Gladstone Solomon. But Solomon was a businessman, not nearly so well placed as Porter to drive home the liberal message. As the government's legal officer, the attorney general had all manner of problems submitted to him for his opinion by the government, by local officials the length and breadth of the colony, by municipal bodies and by individuals. No man was in a better position to know what was going on, or to be widely known. The prominence of his position in the legal system also attracted private clients to him so that his practice at the bar grew with his reputation.

The attorney general's *ex officio* duties in the executive council and in the legislative council widened the range and scope of his involvement in public affairs. In the executive council Porter's role was more political than legal and though the executive council did not meet often or regularly, he was, as attorney general, regularly consulted on political questions. As a legislative councillor he was called upon to draft legislation and to assist in guiding it through the council. Here his knowledge of parliamentary procedure and his impressive oratory singled him out as the leading member and ensured that his views carried great weight when parliamentary institutions were being established in the Cape Colony. His service in the Cape parliament, for long as an *ex officio* member and eventually as an elected representative of Cape Town in the house of assembly, was so distinguished that when responsible government came he was the natural choice as the first prime minister of the colony. The post was offered to him, indeed pressed on him, by the governor but Porter declined to accept it.

1   *Journal*, SAL, Porter papers.

6
Private Life And Social Obligations

Porter had broken away from his strict puritanical upbringing before he left Ireland. At his last meeting with Frances Classon on the day before he set out for the Cape she gave him a little booklet of questions and exhortations which she had compiled over the previous week or two and which she called Aunt Fanny's medley catechism. Directly and by implication it reveals some intimate details about Porter's habits and behaviour. Much as she loved and admired him she felt it necessary to mention some things which 'none except a wife or myself would presume to comment on'. She warned him against picking his teeth or his nose and ears or paring his nails when sitting after dinner, and against 'the slovenly habit' of sitting at his ease with waistcoat unbuttoned, stock off and suspenders loose. She was concerned that he was indulging himself by taking snuff and developing a taste for 'the deadly poison of alcohol'. What worried her most, however, was his neglect of the sabbath and of his religious principles. He was given to reading newspapers, discussing politics and even transacting legal business on Sundays and he was no longer showing the interest he once did in religious controversies. 'Remember', she urged, 'all you have said and done in this cause, and let not your present coldness lead the world to believe you were once a hypocrite'.[1]

Porter lived in the Cape Colony for thirty-four years. For all that time he rarely moved out of Cape Town. He went on circuit twice, in 1840 and in 1847, and he accompanied the governor to the frontier in 1845, but after that he did not see the Eastern Province again until he attended the session of the Cape parliament in Grahamstown in 1864. Towards the end of his career he paid two visits home, one in 1862-3 when he was unwell and overworked, and the other in 1867 after he had retired from the attorney generalship. The truth is, as the Eastern Province politicians said, he was very much a Cape Town man. When he was north of the frontier in 1845 he went to the site of the skirmish between the Trekkers and British troops at Zwartkoppies and was moved to write a few lines of verse for Lynar's amusement:

Swartkoppies look on heaps of stone
And these, again, on Touwfontein
And musing there an hour alone
I wished me at the Kaap again
For riding where the springboks roam
I could not feel myself at home.

Nor did he anywhere else outside of Cape Town.

For their first week in Cape Town, Porter and Lynar lived in the George Hotel, but they found it uncomfortable and full of fleas so they moved to lodgings in Longmarket Street where they had the top floor of a house with three bedrooms, a drawing room, a large lobby and 'something that answers for a pantry', for eleven guineas a month. What they really wanted, however, was a house in the country and after looking at several they settled for one at Rondebosch which was being let by an 'Indian' for seven months. They remained in this area for the rest of their days in the colony. By 1847 they were living in a house called 'Rygersdal', along the Liesbeek river. From there they moved in 1849 to 'Hermitage' at Rondebosch, a house belonging to Rev. George Hough. Four years later they found a permanent home, 'Wolmunster' in Mowbray, a house which is still in existence. Porter's chambers in Cape Town were in St George's Street.[2]

Porter and Lynar lived together and were rarely separated for the whole of their years at the Cape and when Lynar died in 1873 Porter left the colony for good three weeks later. The relationship between them was described by the *Cape Argus* at the time of Lynar's death as 'all but unprecedented in the annals of friendship'.[3] Whether or not it rested on a homosexual basis it is

69

impossible to say. Neither was ever married but Porter came near to being. On 10 August 1846 he wrote an ebullient letter to his half-brother Frank, who was with the Cape volunteers near the Amatolas, telling him that he had proposed to Eliza Smith and had been accepted. Before arranging the wedding day he wanted to know when Frank thought he might get back from the frontier. He confessed to being 'too old for the poor girl' and that there were 'numerous matters regarding a long Dutch connection which I might wish otherwise', but what worried him more was Lynar's reaction. Lynar had taken offence at not having been told about the proposal beforehand and 'the annoyance was considerable for the moment but is now over'.[4] It was not over, however. A fortnight later Lynar wrote to Frank describing subsequent developments. Porter had been induced to seek a 'change of scene' to think things over. He had just returned 'as much depressed as ever.' Meantime Lynar had seen the girl and was convinced that a scheming mother had engineered the situation. 'As to poor Smith, I acquit him of all manoeuvring. But the wife's family have the character of bagging game unerringly in the matrimonial field'. There was no means of knowing what the girl really felt because, as Porter confessed to him, 'a single word other than nonsense had never passed between them' and the girl herself had admitted to Lynar that 'Papa and Mamma had seen such notes as she had written'. One of them, he added, 'I am not sure Mamma did not see before it was written'. So, he persuaded Porter not to write to the girl, as he had promised to do on his return but to confine himself to a business letter to her father which seems to have involved the payment of £2,000.[5] That ended Porter's matrimonial venture.

A few of the letters which Porter wrote to Lynar while on circuit in 1840 begin with the words 'Dearly Beloved', but in character and content they differ in no way from all the other letters he wrote addressed to 'My dear Hugh'. The words may have a special significance, but equally Porter may only be echoing the words of the general confession in the Church of Ireland prayer book, and that would be consistent with his frequent resort to biblical and Shakespearean turns of speech. It is also worth remembering that Lynar was held in affectionate esteem by Porter's relatives and that no murmur of scandal was ever voiced in Cape Town.

Lynar was a contrast to Porter in every way. He was a stout, stumpy man and his personality was very different from Porter's. He was brusque almost to the point of rudeness, gruff and somewhat irascible. He believed in speaking his mind. When a prominent official came to Porter's office to announce his promotion and receive Porter's congratulations Lynar, without lifting his head or interrupting his writing, growled at him 'Never thought much of you'.[6] In later years he and Porter travelled into Cape Town by train and it was a common sight to see them on the way to the station, Porter striding ahead with Lynar a long way behind carrying the lunch basket. Not infrequently Lynar would become involved in some dispute with the stationmaster until Porter came along and quietly settled the matter.[7] Nevertheless, Lynar enjoyed convivial company and was regarded as a good foil to Porter. It fell to his lot to make the practical arrangements: to search for accommodation in the early days, for example, and organise the packing and find furniture and household equipment. He was 'on the figits to have the house and everything else in something like order' when Lady Napier announced her intention of accompanying the governor to dine with them. 'These women have such eyes and in a bachelor's den there must be so many oversights'.[8] As the episode of the marriage proposal shows, Lynar tried to protect Porter from being cheated or imposed upon but he was at heart a kindly man and very charitable, and he is said to have fallen victim himself to many a hard-luck story.

The pattern of Porter's social life at the Cape was set in the first few weeks. He arrived just in time for the Indian ball, one of the highlights of the Cape season, organised by the officers and officials on leave from India, 'yellow-looking men, with ribbons in the button hole'. A few days later he went to the last ball of the season at Sir John Wylde's, attended, like the previous one, by about 300 people. Two or three times a week he was invited to dine — at government house, with Hamilton Ross, with Advocate Cloete, with one or other of the judges, with Colonel Bell, the secretary of government or with the officers of the 72nd Regiment — and if the venue was out of town he would stay the night. The same round of balls and dinners was being followed when Frank Porter arrived in the colony several years later.[9] Church-going was an indispensable part of Victorian life and Porter took an early opportunity of consulting a prominent merchant called Venning, whose family John Scott Porter knew, about which church he should go to, there being no Unitarian church in Cape Town at that time. Dr Adamson of the Scots church, it appeared, was a good and learned man but a poor preacher, Dr Philip the Independent, 'an angel with the Emancipators and Aboriginists, a devil with the Dutch and the Durbanites', preached a very 'pungent' kind of Calvinism, so on the whole he decided to take Venning's advice and try St George's, the Anglican church where Rev. George Hough officiated. Next day, his first Sunday at the Cape, he went to St George's and found the congregation little different from one at home; there were only two coloured people in the church. The clergyman read the service impressively and preached a tolerable, if somewhat verbose, sermon in which he 'handled liberally a topic full of provocatives to illiberality', the duty of churchmen to promote education on high church principles.[10] Most days after finishing work in the office about 4 o'clock he and Lynar went for a walk — on the Lion's Rump, to Green Point, up the Kloof, or, if they were in the country, in their host's grounds. In later years he rode with the Cape Hunt but he had no inclination towards the contemporary passion for shooting game and once 'avowed the monstrous heresy that sport is not a religious duty or to be classed among the highest virtues'.[11]

Although Porter gives every impression of being happy at the Cape from the beginning he did not forget 'the distant and the dear'; he frequently talked about his family and friends in Ireland, he cherished letters from home, he followed the careers of his professional contemporaries in Ireland with great interest and he searched the *Northern Whig*, which was sent to him regularly, for news of familiar people and places — he even blessed the Orangemen when Limavady was mentioned because they had held a demonstration there. He does not seem to have been a great letter writer himself; his stepmother said she was almost as poor a correspondent as he was and she hoped he would write more frequently when Frank told him how glad they were to receive his letters.[12] But if he did not write to his family often he had their welfare at heart. While on circuit in 1840 he learnt from a 'kind, honest, straightforward, in fact characteristic letter of my poor old dad' that he needed £50 to pay a pressing debt. He wrote post-haste to Lynar, 'This he must have, and that at once', and he instructed Lynar on the most expeditious way of transmitting it.[13] After his father's death in 1843 he made his stepmother an allowance of £50 a year,[14] the amount of the salary his father had received as clerk of the synod. He also brought out his youngest half-brother Frank to the Cape, arranged with Hamilton Ross for his entry into Ross's firm and lent him £2,000 to set himself up in business.[15]

Porter's generosity was not confined to his own family. One of the first things he did when he landed at Cape Town was to get a six guinea snuff box for Forster, the captain of the *Sterling*, and have it inscribed 'Gabriel Forster from William Porter as a token of sincere respect and in acknowledgement of much kindness and attention, Cape Town, September 1839'. A couple of days later he presented it to him at a dinner to which he had invited all the passengers who had come out with him.[16] He was on circuit in 1847 when news reached him of the death of a friend at Cape Town. He immediately wrote to Lynar, enclosing a note to the widow, and telling Lynar to provide the money for her comfort at the Cape and her return home, as he would do 'for my own widow did I leave one under similar circumstances'. 'I am not prepared to fix any limit other than her wants', he added.[17] Throughout his career he was always willing to subscribe to any scheme for the relief of distress or the benefit of the colony, and his donations were invariably among the most generous. He was a leading contributor to a relief fund for the victims of the Great Famine in Ireland and secretary of the Starving Irish Committee; at a meeting in 1851 to organise help for those who were suffering in the frontier war he moved the setting up of a committee and subscribed £25; he helped to organise a fund to provide for the widow and three younger children of his old antagonist John Montagu and gave £100; he subscribed £25, as against the £10 of wealthy merchants like Rutherfoord and Ebden, to the Patriotic Fund for the widows and orphans of soldiers killed in the Crimean War; he contributed £25 towards organising a ball on the occasion of the visit of Prince Alfred in 1860, and when the prince laid the foundation stone of a new Sailors' Home and donated £5, he subscribed £25.[18] When the Cape parliament, on his retirement, voted him a pension equal to his full salary he ascertained from the auditor general that the difference between his ordinary pension and the one parliament had awarded him was £480 a year. He then vested the sum of £500 a year in the Board of Public Examiners in Literature and Science, the body established in 1858 as a first step towards promoting university education in the colony, and stipulated that if he died before the board had received £2,500 his executors should make up the deficiency. He laid down one condition 'As the representatives of the whole colony, without distinction, were the men who bestowed upon me the means of usefulness, the educational establishment of the whole colony, without distinction, shall be allowed to compete for whatever prize or prizes the Board may think proper to establish'.[19]

Porter was constantly in the public eye; nothing of any importance took place in Cape Town without his involvement. He regularly attended levees and other functions at government house. He acted as a steward for the subscription balls during the Cape season. As the most highly esteemed orator in the town he was much in demand as a public speaker. When a governor or some other public figure was honoured by a banquet he was invariably called upon to propose the toast, and sometimes more than one toast. Societies and public bodies invited him to address them, and when the colony had a royal visitor in 1860 it was he who delivered the address of welcome. He took a particular interest in cultural and educational matters. He acted as law examiner for the Board of Public Examiners; he was a prime mover in the campaign to establish the University of the Cape of Good Hope in 1873; he was a member of the South African Public Library committee for many years; he was on the council of directors of the South African College and he served on the committee of the South African Literary and Scientific Institution and of the South African Infant Schools. His interests were not confined to the educational sphere, however. He was vice-president of the Sailors' Home and Seamens' Friend Society; a committee member of the Cape of Good Hope Humane Society and the Cape of Good Hope Agricultural Society, a trustee of the Church of England Provident Society and from 1841 president of the Cape of Good Hope Savings Bank, 'an institution devoted to the protection, assistance and encouragement of the deserving poor'.[20] He was always on *ad hoc* committees like the ones set up to organise an exhibition of fine arts in Cape Town, to arrange for Cape exhibits at the Great Exhibition of 1851 and the Paris Exhibition of 1854, to manage the Patriotic Fund, to make a presentation to David Livingstone and to relieve distress after a disastrous gale in Table Bay in 1865. During the frontier war of 1846-47 he joined the Cape volunteers and became commanding officer. In 1857 he organised and became captain of the Cape Town volunteer cavalry, known as the Sparklers because of their striking uniform. In this capacity he acted as aide-de-camp to Prince Alfred in 1860. He was involved as well in the business life of the town. He was a director of the Cape Commercial Bank and chairman of the board of directors of the Cape of Good Hope Gas Light Company.

Both Porter, and, to a lesser extent, Lynar made a lot of money at the Cape. In spite of his relatively modest salary, first as clerk in the attorney general's office and then as clerk of the peace of Cape Town and at times acting resident magistrate, Lynar left over £15,000 when he died. Successful speculation was the source of his wealth: with other securities, he left shares in seven banks and thirteen insurance companies. The bulk of his fortune he bequeathed to members of the Porter and Classon families, Porter himself, 'to whom', in Lynar's words, 'I owe it that I possess anything to bequeath', having refused absolutely 'to take back what I consider to be his own'. But he also made the generous bequest of £400 to the South African Public Library and £200 each to the Sailors' Home, the Ladies Benevolent Society and the Cape Town Dispensary. Porter, who, in addition to his salary as attorney general, had a lucrative private practice and substantial investments, accumulated a very large fortune, considerably in excess of £56,000 when he died.[21]

When Porter was going on leave in 1862 a public meeting in Cape Town drew up an address, signed by 1,410 people, asking him to have his portrait painted in Britain for presentation to the South African Public Library. Porter expressed the wish, however, that the money they intended to spend on a portrait should be used instead to purchase books for the library. This was done, and the books form what is still known as the Porter Collection. His departure in May 1862 was the occasion for a great demonstration of respect. Resolutions of sympathy and good wishes signed by all the leading inhabitants, Dutch and English, came in from remote districts, including one from 'a humble native congregation', and when he boarded the *Camperdown* he was 'escorted by bands of music and all the volunteers of Cape Town'. On his return in December 1863 he was 'met with a reception as cordial as it was sincere; all classes and colours welcome his return'. Country dwellers like the residents of Malmesbury who 'were precluded from forming part of the throng of friends who greeted you on the decks of the *Cambrian*' sent addresses of welcome. His resignation in 1865 evoked another spate of addresses from places as remote as Clanwilliam, and here again Dutch and English joined in the tributes.[22] An official honour was conferred on him in November 1872 when he became a Companion of the Order of St Michael and St George, having on previous occasions refused a knighthood. He left Cape Town for the last time on the morning of 16 August 1873, after the ship had been delayed from the previous day by a fierce gale, but in spite of the driving rain and the gusty wind a large number of people assembled at the docks to see him off. That morning the Cape Town papers carried a notice he had inserted announcing his intention to retire from public life. They also paid glowing tributes to him and expressed the hope that he would soon return, for, as one of them said, 'South Africa can ill spare her greatest citizen and her only orator'.[23]

1   Aunt Fanny's medley catechism, 16 June 1839, SAL, Porter papers.
2   Journal, ibid; *Cape almanac*, 1845-56; *SAAM*, 2 July 1853.
3   *Argus*, 24 July 1873.
4   Porter to Frank Porter, 10 August 1846, SAL, Porter papers.
5   Lynar to same, 24 August 1846, ibid.
6   A. W. Cole, 'Reminiscences of Cape bar', in *Cape Law Journal*, 1888, V. 1-12.
7   V. Salmson, *My reminiscences*, p.35.
8   Lynar to Frank Porter, 9 March 1844, SAL, Porter papers.
9   Frank Porter's diary, April 1845-January 1846, ibid.
10   Journal, ibid.
11   A. F. Hattersley, *An illustrated social history*, p.212; GTJ, 16 July 1869.
12   Eliza Porter to Frank Porter, 21 March (1844), 20 May 1845, SAL, Porter papers.
13   Porter to Lynar, 24 October 1840 ibid.
14   Frank Porter's diary; Eliza Porter to Frank Porter, 4 November. 1844,ibid.
15   Porter to same, 10 March 1844; Lynar to same, 29 October 1844, ibid.
16   Journal, ibid.

17 Porter to Lynar, 15 October 1847, ibid.
18 *Cape Monitor*, 31 July 1851, 4 February, 30 December 1854, 27 January 1855; *Argus*, 12 July, 20 September 1860.
19 *GTJ*, 18 October 1865; M. Boucher, *Spes in arduis*, pp.9-14.
20 Resolution re Porter adopted at general meeting of Savings Bank Society, 29 March 1862, made available by Sir Andrew Horsburgh-Porter.
21 CA, Will of Hugh Lynar; will of William Porter; Argus, 12 August 1873; GTJ, 28 July 1873.
22 J. Purves (ed), *Letters by Lady Duff Gordon*, p.162; *SAAM*, 14 December 1863; Addresses made available by Sir Andrew Horsburgh-Porter.

7

The Attorney General

Porter was the second attorney general of the Cape Colony. His predecessor, Anthony Oliphant, was a Scots lawyer who had been appointed when the office was created in 1827 as part of the reorganisation of the judicial system. He was a very different man from the industrious and conscientious Porter. Oliphant, in Porter's words, 'took the world easy'. When business got too pressing, Porter was told, he and his clerk used to give up trying to cope with it and do nothing but smoke cigars for a day or two. Next to smoking cigars his chief pleasure in life was attending the numerous auctions in Cape Town and buying rubbish which he never put to any use. Confirmation of Oliphant's easygoing methods is to be found in the brevity of his entries in the attorney general's letter book; in eight years he did not succeed in filling a single folio volume. Porter, by contrast, normally used up a volume in a couple of years. Porter was astonished by the state of the attorney general's office. The floor and tables were so dirty, he said, that 'you would imagine all the dirty work in the colony was done in the attorney general's office'. An Irishman might have planted potatoes in the deep dust which covered everything. There was not a chair on which it was safe to sit down, for Oliphant had strained them all by his 'American habit' of swinging back and forward while smoking his cigars. One of Porter's first resolves was to get something done about the office.

His main concern, however, was to have Lynar installed as his clerk.[1] The establishment consisted of the attorney general himself, a clerk and a messenger. The clerkship was held by a man called Eaton, but Musgrave, who had acted as attorney general during the interregnum, was willing to recommend him for a clerkship of the peace. At first the governor appeared to agree but next day Porter was informed by the colonial secretary, Colonel Bell, that only the judges had the right to appoint their own clerks. Porter disputed this ruling strongly and threatened to appeal to the home government. In view of the conciliatory attitude adopted by the governor and the colonial secretary he decided, however, to bide his time. Within the month the governor called at his office and offered Eaton the clerkship of the peace at Grahamstown. This cleared the way for Lynar's appointment to the post which, as Porter said, suited them better than one with a higher salary[2] because they would be perpetually together. For many years they worked not only in the same office but on opposite sides of the same table.

Porter made his first appearance in court as attorney general on 2 October 1839. For the occasion he put on a fine white stock he had got in London for his reception by the queen and a set of the imposing bands worn at the English bar. His silk gown, 'a superior article', completed his attire, for wigs had been discarded by judges and advocates alike some six years before. His seat in court was a sort of armchair, 'or rather a seat like one of those in the Birmingham and London Railway carriages', in the centre of the advocates' bench, railed off from the other advocates. The only business was an application for bail before the chief justice, Sir John Wylde, and Mr Justice Kekewich. After a rambling address the chief justice asked for Porter's opinion which he gave at some length, quoting a good many authorities, both Scottish and English.[3]

As attorney general Porter had the twofold role of legal adviser to the government and public prosecutor, responsible for the conduct of all criminal proceedings. The two functions, Porter said, 'although united in the same person, should be regarded as distinct, and are functions which, were theoretical perfection alone consulted, would never be combined'.[4] Some of the matters referred to him as law adviser by the governor and the colonial secretary were of the same kind as those which came to

FOR CALCUTTA.

FREIGHT AND PASSAGE.

THE fine fast-sailing Barque *"Sterling,"* A. 1, 360 Tons, G. FORSTER, Master, will Sail on *Thursday next*, the 10th instant, weather permitting: has some of her superior Accommodations vacant, and offers an excellent opportunity for the conveyance of Horses. — For Particulars, apply to Capt. G. FORSTER, on board, or to
L. TWENTYMAN & Co.

Top: Kingstown Pier in 1834. It was from here, five years later, that Porter set out on the first stage of his journey to the Cape.

Bottom: The *Sterling* soliciting custom prior to continuing her voyage to Calcutta in October 1839.

Above right: Porter in later life
Above: Porter as an older man

Right: Adam Kok.
Captain or chief of the Griquas.
He was, said Porter, 'nearly black, with the
negro features beautifully developed, with
a cunning little eye and his organs
of eating strongly marked'.

The Heerengracht, Cape Town circa 1840, later renamed Adderley Street. In the foreground left is the Commercial Exchange, centre, the spire of the Groote Kerk and , showing above the houses on the right, the spire of St George's Church.

St George's Street, Cape Town, where Porter had his chambers, with St George's Church, the first church Porter attended in Cape Town.

Wolmunster at Mowbray in
Cape Town. This was Porter's
home from 1853 until he left
the Cape.

Old Supreme Court,
Cape Town as it was in
Porter's day.

him as public prosecutor but others had political as well as legal implications. Under the criminal procedure in the colony Porter, as attorney general, had the uncontrolled and independent power of prosecuting for all crime. When a report of the proceedings at a preliminary examination in the court of the resident magistrate in a district had been forwarded to him he decided whether or not to prosecute. If the offence was a minor one the case was remitted to the magistrate's court for trial without a jury. More serious cases were submitted to a grand jury in the Cape District and tried in the supreme court, where the attorney general prosecuted in person; elsewhere the case went directly for trial by the circuit judge and a jury, and the clerk of the peace for the district acted as the attorney general's deputy. In addition to this normal flow of work Porter, as attorney general, received a wide variety of appeals and complaints from individuals and public bodies. Some people, he once said, seemed to regard the attorney general as a kind of general attorney bound to act for anybody who chose to require his services.[5]

The law which he had to administer was Roman-Dutch law, a system to which he 'had not been bred', but within a remarkably short time he had made himself familiar with it. He read *The institutes of Justinian* and Van der Linden's *Koopman's handboek* on the way out to the Cape and he was quoting Roman-Dutch authorities in the supreme court two months after his arrival in the colony.[6] He came to believe that Roman-Dutch law challenged comparison with any other system of jurisprudence the world had ever seen. As part of his adaptation to the new system he acquired a working knowledge of Dutch.

The attorney general had the right to practise at the Cape bar in cases where the crown was not involved. Porter was admitted as an advocate of the supreme court on 12 October 1839, after a brush with chief justice Sir John Wylde who wanted him to support his application with an affidavit from his friends Hanna and Lynar, vouching for his legal standing. Here, as in the case of the clerkship, Porter felt he owed it to himself and his office to make a stand. A member of the Irish bar, appointed by the British government as a colonial attorney general, should not require any further authentication. Faced with a firm refusal to comply with their suggestion, the chief justice and his colleague Mr Justice Kekewich gave way. Within a short time Porter was being briefed, either alone or with some other leading counsel, in almost every civil action of importance. In the first ten years he was involved in about a hundred major cases and when he was granted leave of absence in 1862 it was said that he enjoyed by far the largest share of private practice at the bar.[7]

Porter made a good impression in the country districts by going on circuit at the earliest possible opportunity, the more so as Oliphant had never troubled to go. Between mid-September and mid-November 1840 he accompanied Chief Justice Wylde, three fellow advocates and an interpreter on the circuit which took them to Colesberg by Stellenbosch, Beaufort West and Graaff Reinet, then by Cradock and Somerset East to Grahamstown, then to Uitenhage, then by Port Elizabeth and the Long Kloof to George, and thence back to Cape Town by Swellendam. From Porter's lively account of their journey a picture emerges of the highlights and hazards of life on circuit. On the first day's ride to Stellenbosch, Porter 'lost some leather' but Sir John Wylde gave him a plaster and he was soon 'case-hardened'. After spending two nights on the journey they got to Graaff Reinet where they had a great many cases. Graaff Reinet was a pretty village but Porter had little good to say of Colesberg. Never in his life had he been so bitten by bugs. On their arrival and departure they were saluted by gunfire, a foolish waste of gunpowder in Porter's opinion: it should have been used to blow the place up. The road to Cradock took them through fine sheep country but nearly all the sheep were the Cape breed. When Porter on three occasions asked farmers why they did not try wool sheep he got the same reply, that it was troublesome to shear them. 'Trouble is a thing these gentlemen are not fond of', he concluded. The first night they stayed at Hemming's Fontein with a family called van der Walt who seemed unwilling or unable to offer them much hospitality. Sir John had to sleep in his wagon, Ebden, van Ryneveld, Edward Wylde and the interpreter, Roselt 'sheepskinned it' on the floor and Porter himself spent the night with his sheepskin spread over a bed with a corded bottom so that his body was cut into small squares next morning. The second night they spent comfortably at a farm belonging to Gilfillan, the resident magistrate of Cradock, where they were told there were plenty of lions. Next day a morning ride under a blazing sun brought them to Cradock where they had excellent accommodation in the best house in the town. The court completed its business in two days and on the Sunday morning Porter heard two sermons, a good one from the Independent minister and a bad one from the Dutch Reformed minister. The next stage of their journey to Somerset took them over the formidable Ganna Hoek which they negotiated with difficulty by wagon with teams of oxen and they did not reach their stopping place — Jordaan's — till 8 o'clock at night.[8] Supper Porter did not enjoy because the servants who served it 'were enough to turn the stomach of a horse'. Nor did they have a comfortable night. Porter's bed was a foot and a half too short and the bedclothes were filthy dirty. Ebden and Wylde shared his room, while van Ryneveld and Roselt settled for the floor of the hall outside, where they had to endure the chatter of a crowd of Khoikhoi women for most of the night. Even the sight of van Ryneveld sitting up in his red nightcap and solemnly commanding them to be gone had no effect; one of them merely told him to lie down and go to sleep and not to disturb himself on their account. Next day the resident magistrate of Somerset met them about an hour out of the town. They admired the site and the surrounding scenery but found the town itself paltry, the houses few and far between, badly built and ill-cared for. But they were comfortably lodged with the widow of a missionary. There were few cases to detain them and on the third day they set out for Grahamstown. Here Porter was treated 'like the son of an Irish king'. He was the guest of honour at a dinner attended by all the leading citizens. At Uitenhage, their next stopping place, they were occupied for five days. From there they went to Port Elizabeth where they spent the night. Next day, after eleven hours of hard riding, they got to Jagersbos where they had comfortable quarters and abundant food with a 'fat, good-humoured hostess, a perfect lump of living laughter'. After a day's rest they went on to Field Commandant Raademeyer's in the Long Kloof where they spent the night very comfortably.[9] From here van Ryneveld and Ebden set off next morning on a race to George to get briefs. An all-day ride through the Long Kloof brought the rest of the party to Gauskraal where they passed the night with a decent but dirty family, the van Rensberghs. Three hours after setting out next morning they reached the base of Cradock Kloof. Only the horsemen attempted the crossing, the wagons being sent by the Devil's Kop. 'All I had ever heard or read of this infernal road', Porter wrote, 'proved nothing to the horrible reality. It would require a goat of some activity to clamber over it with anything like ease'. To complete their discomfort they encountered a thunderstorm before they reached George and the chief justice was thrown from his horse on the slippery road, 'burying his nose for some depth in the soft clay'. They reached their lodgings dripping wet and Porter had to go to bed until his clothes dried. Three days disposed of the court's business and on the following morning they set out for home. By the time they reached Swellendam they were in relaxed mood. In a note, 'Given at Swellendam at 12 o'clock at night under our hand (a little unsteady)' Porter informed Lynar 'We have dined out and drank what seemed unto us good of the juice of the grape'.

One way or another Porter was fully occupied while on circuit. He was heavily involved in cases at Graaff Reinet and came out of court 'tired and exhausted beyond measure'. In addition he was appealed to about market regulations by contending parties in the municipality. At Colesberg he heard a report about the new colony in Natal from Field Cornet Joubert who had been sent on a mission there the previous year. According to him the volksraad was feeble and the people 'a rope of sand'. Religious bickering had broken out over the respective merits of the old psalm book and the new hymn book and the precise meaning of the texts in the Old Testament in which all parties agreed that Port Natal was spoken of. Rust was killing the crops and rank grass the sheep, the people were indolent and everything was going wrong. Without a firm and settled government the venture would fail. Porter suspected that the report was substantially accurate. At Cradock, he had only a couple of cases. Before he left the town he spoke to Blair, the acting clerk of the peace, about the desirability of taking steps to make himself less unpopular than he was. At Jordaan's place, on the way to Somerset, Porter had scarcely got his foot out of the stirrup when he was approached by a Prussian, the caretaker of one of Stockenstrom's sheep farms in the neighbourhood, with a request for an opinion.[10] His wife refused to join him in Africa and he wanted to know if he might marry again. Knowing that a divorce was out of the question for financial reasons Porter told him that if his conscience allowed him to remarry he saw no legal danger of a prosecution. At Somerset Porter had two civil cases, one for libel and the other a defamation case in which a young man charged an old lady with saying that he went to bed with a black woman. 'Whether or not she says that he remained there just ten minutes I am not instructed', he commented. At Grahamstown Porter had a busy and profitable time. Of the £132.19s. which he forwarded to Lynar in Cape Town £95 represented fees earned at Grahamstown. In Uitenhage he was engaged, to the exclusion of legal business, in working with Sir George Napier on the treaties which the governor was proposing to conclude with the tribes beyond the frontier. Finally, at George, he had to investigate a charge of receiving money illegally, made by a field cornet against the clerk of the civil commissioner.[11]

Porter's purpose in going on circuit was to acquaint himself with conditions in the interior, but his journey had the additional effect of bringing him into contact with officials and public figures in the remote parts of the colony and establishing at an early stage of his career a personal relationship which proved to be significant.

The impression which he made and the respect which he won persisted in a part of the colony where his views on frontier affairs, labour relations and separatism were far from popular. When he retired in 1865 the *Grahamstown Journal* went so far as to admit that, though he was a Western man, 'Eastern men can parly with Mr Porter without insisting upon wearing armour and double cocking their pistols during the interview'.[12]

The dual role of attorney general and private advocate created a problem for Porter when the capacity in which he was consulted was not clear. When, for example, he was asked if a British subject who had already married a Griqua woman in Griqualand could legally marry again in the colony he noted that from one point of view the question was merely an abstract point of law upon which, as an advocate, he could properly accept a fee for his opinion, but from another point of view it could be regarded as virtually asking whether or not, as public prosecutor, he would proceed against the man if he remarried. In this case, as in all similar cases, he refused to accept a fee because, he said, he wished to avoid all shadow of interference between his private practice and his public duty.[13] There also could be no question of accepting a fee when he was privately consulted on a public issue. He returned a sovereign to a man who complained of unjust treatment, because the matter fell clearly within the line of his public duty.[14] He explained to the municipal commissioners of Grahamstown that he could not advise them professionally and accept 'the ordinary inducement which generally puts lawyers into motion', because in this case the question they were putting to him would, in due course, come before him in his capacity as a member of the executive council.[15] The municipal commissioners of Swellendam were also told that they should not have marked their letter to him 'On Her Majesty's Service' because it was not on a public matter.[16] Yet on each of these occasions he proceeded to give his opinion on the problem laid before him. That was Porter's normal practice. As in duty bound he always declined to advise private individuals on any matter involved in a public prosecution, though he never failed to draw the resident magistrate's attention to anything they had brought to his notice.[17] Apart from that, he made every possible effort to help those who sought his aid; often going to considerable trouble. He spent a whole morning looking up the law about transfer on behalf of a poor man and when he was asked by a man whose daughter had been accused of theft and subsequently proved to be innocent if she could prosecute the person who had given false information about her Porter wrote a three-page letter setting out the possible procedures and advising him to find a competent lawyer and show him the attorney general's letter.[18]

Porter as attorney general was consulted by people beyond the frontier as well. To such approaches he responded in the same spirit as he did to those from within the colony. He would gladly have given his opinion without a fee to the Berlin Mission at Bethany, 'so unpretending, earnest and non-political a mission', had not his official position precluded him from advising anyone except the governor on the public issue they raised.[19] In reply to an inquiry from Potchestroom in 1854 as to whether the Boers had any legal redress for what they regarded as libels on them in the newspapers he gave it as his opinion that the true redress, if not the only one, in such cases was to be sought not in prosecution in courts of law but in an appeal through the press, 'to the fairness and justice of mankind'.[20] He also gave the attorney general of the Orange Free State his views on a legal problem, not as an official opinion but as 'the thoughts of one legal practitioner placed before another', with an apology that lack of time, lack of Dutch and lack of learning prevented him from being of more help.[21] Porter's reputation and the esteem in which he was held in no small measure stemmed from his readiness to respond to approaches from all quarters.

A feature of many of the opinions which Porter gave officially and unofficially was the humanity and concern for the individual which characterised them. Both are frequently evident in the views he expressed in cases concerning the black and coloured peoples (see Chapter 8). In the numerous cases about illegal affinity between partners in a marriage, or people contemplating marriage, which came before him he always took the line that the happiness and social acceptability of the couple should be put before a strict adherence to the legal position. It was desirable to give 'the social function of the marriage ceremony' to such people and though the offspring of such a marriage could not be other than illegitimate the ceremony would 'prevent them from being so reputed'. Any clergyman who performed such a ceremony was assured that he had nothing to fear from the public prosecutor.[22] A minister in Uitenhage who had married a couple whom he subsequently found were within the prohibited degree of relationship was advised not to jeopardise the welfare of the family by doing all that he had the power to do, namely making ministerial remonstrances. For his part, Porter, in the circumstances, would decline to consider the legal aspects of the affinity.[23] Again, having pronounced, at the behest of Rev. Heavyside of Grahamstown, that one clergyman was justified in declining to marry a couple he tartly refused to go further and declare invalid their marriage by another clergyman. The laws of the colony did not come out of his mouth, he said. Only the judges could decide such a question. So far as he was concerned he had 'an individual repugnance' to giving speculative opinions on questions of such extreme delicacy as whether a woman was a wife or concubine and whether her children were legitimate or bastards. In another case where a little girl had been assaulted he was loath to subject the child to the ordeal of giving evidence in court, especially against the parents' wishes. Only if those on the spot decided that she could tell her story without great distress should the trial go ahead. If it did, he outlined the minimum evidence that would be needed from her to secure a conviction.[24] He constantly advised the offering of compensation to avoid people becoming involved in legal proceedings and when, in one case, he felt it necessary to fix at £50 the compensation which a clergyman should pay for injuring a child's hand — after the father had brought her to the attorney general's office — he wrote, 'I am sure that the worldly wealth of a gentleman in your position is not likely to be such that the payment of £50 can be a matter of indifference. I wish I could in justice name some smaller sum'.[25]

Another of Porter's qualities as attorney general was his con-scientiousness in the discharge of his duties. He was punctilious in giving reasons, often at length, for the decisions he reached, he kept a close watch for irregularities in the sentences imposed by resident magistrates for minor offences like drunkenness, he insisted on full details in returns from resident magistrates and clerks of the peace and he administered sharp rebukes to any of them who transgressed, even to the extent of having bad Engl-ish or bad spelling in their reports.

As early as 1844, in a letter urging his younger half-brother Frank to come to the Cape, Porter wrote, 'Come out to me and ask for the attorney general's office. Every coolie knows it'.[26] An important factor contributing to Porter's influence was the fact that everybody knew him; he became an institution as attorney general. He held the office for an exceptionally long period, twenty-six years, far longer than any other senior official of his day at the Cape. The question naturally arises why a man who was highly thought of not only at the Cape but in the colonial office should have remained in the same post for so many years. It was by his own choice. Within a couple of months of his arri-val the chief justice expressed the wish to have him as a col-league on the bench. Porter disclaimed any interest in a judge-ship but he noted privately that if he were to move to the bench it would have to be the chief justiceship.[27] He was offered the first vacancy that occurred on the Cape bench, in 1843, but refused to accept it, though the governor, Sir George Napier, would have 'felt proud' to recommend 'that able and talented officer'.[28] Some years later, in 1855, when news of Chief Justice Wylde's illness reached Rev. John Scott Porter in Belfast, he wrote to the prime minister, Lord Palmerston, pressing his brother's claims to the office. His letter evoked a striking tribute from Herman Merivale, the under-secretary at the colonial office. 'Mr Porter', he wrote,

> is one of the ablest, perhaps first among the ablest legal officers under this department. His reports etc. on important constitutional points connected with South African affairs have been many times printed for parliament and referred to as high authorities in the discussions which have taken place both in and out of parliament. He was substantially (under Lord Grey's direction) the framer of the present Cape constitution and it was a task of no common difficulty.... I have thought it right to minute at once my own opinion of Mr Porter's eminent qualifications and claims on government.[29]

A year later John Scott Porter returned to the attack in a strongly worded letter to the colonial secretary, Henry Labouchère. His brother's distance from the home government and utter aversion to urge or even mention his claims to promotion must, he presumed, explain the government's neglect of him, but he believed that the history of the British empire afforded no other example of an attorney general continuing in office for seventeen years without being promoted.[30] All this went on without Porter's knowledge; but when the chief justiceship eventually became vacant it was offered to him as the person who had 'undoubtedly the best claim to it'. Porter positively refused to accept the appointment 'having', as Sir George Grey reported to the colonial secretary, 'better satisfaction to remain in his present position'.[31] That was the crux of the matter; the attorney generalship at the Cape was an office of great importance not only in the legal but in the political sphere. It was, as Mr Justice Watermeyer wrote to the governor at the time of Porter's retirement, more important than any judicial position in the colony. 'The attorney general has more power for good and evil and more serious responsibilities than even the chief justice'.[32] And Wodehouse agreed that the office was even more important politically than legally under the existing constitution. Besides, there was no financial inducement. To exchange the attorney general's salary of £1,200 for a puisne judgeship at £1,500 or even the chief justiceship at £2,000, would not have compensated Porter for the loss of his private practice. Sir Philip Wodehouse estimated that the office, with the practice, was worth at least £2,000 or £2,500 a year.[33] One other consideration may have weighed with him; there is a tradition in the Porter family[34] that he refused a judgeship because he could not have brought himself to impose the death sentence. Certainly towards the end of his career he did introduce a bill to abolish capital punishment. Perhaps because he was so obviously disinterested himself, Porter's recommendation of others for the bench carried great weight. Sir George Grey offered a judgeship to J. C. Brand in 1855 on the strength of the attorney general's opinion that he was the best lawyer in the colony not on the bench and as good as any on the bench.[35]

Great as were Porter's services to the Cape Colony they did not include an outstanding contribution in the legal sphere. He was not a brilliant lawyer, but he was a learned one. He acquired a sound knowledge of Roman-Dutch law; he had sufficient fluency in Dutch to use it and to quote Dutch authorities, though he always apologised for his pronunciation; he knew enough French to read French books and to cite legal authorities in French, again apologising for his bad accent; he had a thorough knowledge of Latin; and he was very widely read in history and in English literature. He had an immense capacity for work and, until towards the end of his career, great physical stamina. His greatest forensic assets were his oratorial gifts, his melodious voice and his commanding presence.[36] He made no major literary contribution to legal studies but on Mr Justice Menzies' death he bought his manuscript reports on cases decided by the supreme court with a view to publishing them.[37] They were subsequently edited by Porter's protégé, James Buchanan, and published in three volumes in 1870. Porter also wrote a foreword to Hercules Tennant's *The notary's manual*, praising it as accurate, succinct and comprehensive, and particularly useful to persons, who, like himself, knew little Dutch.[38] Porter had a reputation as an advocate for fairness in his presentation of a case and for an almost judicial impartiality in summing up. At the treason trial of Andries Botha, field cornet of the Kat River Settlement, for involvement in the 1851 rebellion the defence counsel paid tribute to Porter for his extreme liberality towards the prisoner.[39] The speaker of the house of assembly, himself a lawyer, declared in his speech at Porter's retirement that he had seen Porter acting as an arbitrator between his own client and his adversary thereby succeeding in doing justice to both, and had seen him censuring his own client. Porter himself said that he had been sent to the colony to prosecute crime, not to persecute. Nevertheless, his habit of examining a question from every angle and his tendency to indecisiveness militated against his success as an advocate.

Porter's retirement from the attorney generalship was the occasion for a remarkable tribute to him by the Cape parliament. On 21 August 1865 the members of the house of assembly stood to receive him and the speaker delivered a eulogy. A week later in the legislative council a motion of appreciation of his services was moved and seconded by two of the foremost Eastern Province members, Godlonton and Wood, whose political views were poles apart from Porter's.[40] The two houses then combined to pass unanimously an act conferring on him a pension equal to the full salary of his office.

1   Providing for relatives and friends seems to have been a common practice among legal and administrative officials at the Cape; Chief Justice Wylde had four sons in the Cape civil service, Secretary Montagu two, Treasurer Rivers and Collector Field one each.
2   The salary was £150 a year. PRO, CO/53/77.
3   Journal, SAL, Porter papers.
4   Rpts, 1843-6, p.301, CA, AG 2617.
5   Journal, SAL, Porter papers.
6   Notes on Porter's cases in supreme court, 1839-49, CA, Kilpin papers.
7   *Argus*, 6 May 1862.
8   W. G. Jordaan, field cornet of Zwager's Hoek in the division of Somerset.
9   J. J. Rodemeyer, one of the two field commandants in the division of George and a justice of the peace.
10 Sir Andries Stockenstrom, landowner, official and politician, was lieutenant governor of the Eastern Province from 1836 to 1839.
11 Porter to Lynar, 22 September, 4 October, 7 October, 24 October, 28 October, 7 November, 9 November 1840, SAL, Porter papers.
12 *GTJ*, 13 November 1865.
13 LB, 1847-51, p.45, CA, AG 2158.
14 LB, 1830-47, p.165, CA, AG 2157.
15 Ibid., p.126.
16 LB, 1855-7, p.118-20, CA, AG 2161.
17 LB, 1847-51, p.262, CA, AG 2158.
18 Ibid., pp.31-4; Journal, SAL, Porter papers.
19 LB, 1851-3, pp.229-300, CA, AG 2159.
20 LB, 1853-5, pp.340-1, CA, AG 2160.
21 LB, 1855-7, pp.252-3, CA, AG 2161.
22 LB, 1853-5, pp.203-4, 344, CA, AG 2160.
23 Rpts, 1841-3, pp.4-5, CA, AG 2616.
24 LB, 1855-7, pp.47-8, CA, AG 2161.
25 LB, 1861-4, pp.81-2, CA, AG 2164.
26 Porter to Frank Porter, 10 March 1844, SAL, Porter papers.
27 Journal, SAL, Porter papers.
28 Napier to Lord Stanley, 28 Apr 1843, PRO, CO 48/229/182-5.
29 J. S. Porter to Lord Palmerston, 3 November 1855 and note by Herman Merivale, 8 November 1855, PRO, CO 48/371/457-8.
30 Same to H. Labouchere, 4 November 1856, PRO, CO 48/379/569-71.
31 Grey to same, 31 July 1857, PRO, CO 48/382/349-57.
32 E. B. Watermeyer to Wodehouse, 8 June 1865, PRO, CO 48/427/389-93; Wodehouse to Cardwell, 9 June 1865, ibid, ff 389-93.
33 Wodehouse to Edward Cardwell, 9 June 1865, COL, A3C15, Private correspondence of Wodehouse.
34 Information from the late Mrs Margot Vernon and Mr Eric Porter.

35 Grey to J. C. Brand, 16 July 1855, PRO, CO 48/367/306-7.
36 A. W. Cole, Reminiscences, pp.9, 58.
37 A. F. Hattersley, Social history, p.73.
38 Hercules Tennant, *The notary's manual*, Preface.
39 *Cape Monitor*, 22 May 1852.
40 *GTJ*, 28 August, 4 September 1865.

8
Porter In A Multi-Racial Society

In his official capacity Porter was constantly called upon to formulate opinions and prescribe actions on matters concerning the coloured population of the colony and the black peoples within and beyond its boundaries. In doing so he was often involved as well with the farmers, especially the frontier farmers, and the emigrant Boers who were frequently in conflict with the black and coloured people. Furthermore, as a Cape Town resident, many of his social and professional associates were Dutch-speaking colonists, while his pro-western outlook and sympathies were resented by the British settlers of the Eastern Province.

To the complex situation in which he found himself Porter brought certain basic convictions. He always described himself as an Irishman, but like his fellow liberals in Ulster he strongly supported the political union with Britain and he had a profound respect for England which he regarded as the home of freedom, 'the chief of nations'. 'When I reflect,' he told a colonial audience, 'upon all that England is doing and has already done, upon the great people she has bred in America, upon the mighty empire she is founding in Australia, upon her wonderful history from first to last I see something that awes and elevates my mind and feel thankful that I live under the government of the Anglo-Saxon race'.

But he had experienced too much racial tension in Ireland to be blind to the sensitivities of the other European component of the colony's population. While eulogising the English he was careful to stress his admiration for the inhabitants of French and Teutonic extraction. 'Trojans and Tyrians are all the same to me'.[1] Indeed, he was very much averse to differentiation and

95

antagonism between the two communities. The terms Dutch and English should be avoided wherever possible, he said, and it was his sincere wish that the distinction which they denoted should cease to exist.

Towards that end he treated the old colonists and their language with respect. Soon after his arrival in the colony he took lessons in Dutch and acquired what he modestly called a smattering of the language. For those who were disposed to laugh at colonists of the old stock who expressed themselves awkwardly in English he had the utmost contempt; wit at the expense of people who made the effort to use a language they were not born to was very misplaced. He also believed that a lack of command of English need not prevent a man from being a useful member of the Cape parliament. When pressure was being exerted for the introduction of English labourers to ease the labour shortage he argued that they would never be acceptable to the Boers because they differed too profoundly in way of life, way of living, manners and customs. The Boer, 'with his allodial notion of his position as a landowner', could never work with 'a bare-breeched fellow brought in the other day at government expense', who would try to teach him his business. It was idle to call this prejudice and to assume that it would disappear, 'for there are prejudices too deeply implanted to be easily eradicated'.[2] Though many of the Boers, in his opinion, were as politically unsophisticated as the coloured man he insisted on a low franchise qualification when representative government was being introduced, for he had great hopes of the new political system breaking down barriers. 'When the Dutch majority, long depressed, shall have got over the temporary elation of acquiring power, and the English minority shall have got over, in like manner, their temporary mortification at being less influential than before, the fusion of race, and colour, and language which is undoubtedly in progress will be promoted and the peace and prosperity of the colony, though not, perhaps, till after many follies and failures, be ultimately advanced'.[3]

In his attitude to the coloured and black population Porter was guided by the New Light principles he had imbibed in the earlier part of his career. He had come to the colony, he said, with 'an unspeakable hatred of oppression of every kind'.[4] He believed that progress could most surely be achieved by cultivating personal responsibility and initiative. He took for granted the superiority of the civilisation to which he belonged. He was, he said, very sceptical of the existence of noble savages anywhere, and he considered that those 'who deemed that, in regard to communities of men, their moral excellence might be high while their civilisation was very low were labouring under a generous delusion'. For himself, he had 'a very humble estimate of the Kafir character'. Nevertheless he was shocked by the sentiments of men on the Cape eastern frontier and in the British house of commons who advocated the extermination of the blacks to make way for white colonists. 'This profound contempt of colour, and lofty pride of race', he said, 'contains within it the concentrated essence and active principle of all the tyranny and oppression which white has ever exercised over black'.[5] In their practical application these views moved Porter not merely to insist on absolute equality before the law and protection against exploitation and maltreatment, but also to open the way for advancement to those inhabitants of the colony who gave evidence of a willingness to adopt European civilisation and values. On the other hand, his experience of Irish evangelical fervour made him distrustful of the impartiality of missionaries and philanthropists, and he saw nothing to admire in the way of life of the peoples beyond the range of colonial influence. Yet even they deserved protection from annihilation and exploitation by superior European forces. The frontier wars of 1846-47 and 1850-53 and the rebellion of the Kat River Khoikhoi hardened his views about uncivilised peoples but did not shake his faith in the justice and wisdom of the racial policy being pursued within the colony.

As attorney general, Porter had occasion repeatedly to assert the principle of equality before the law. Often the issue arose out of servants' grievances against masters. In such cases Porter followed a consistent line. Employers had to be taught that they could not inflict degrading punishments on their coloured servants with impunity. They must be made to realise that as 'all flesh stands equal before God, so likewise it stands before the law of this colony'.[6] When a field cornet and a farmer in the Uitenhage district were each sentenced to a month's imprisonment for flogging a black servant, Porter expressed the opinion that the sentence would not fail to produce very beneficial results in a portion of the colony in which, at least amongst the white part of the population, the restraints of law appeared to be very little regarded;[7] and in another assault case he advised against remitting the fine of a Burgersdorp farmer because of the need to restrain the tendency of farmers in certain quarters to commit assaults upon their servants, particularly black ones.[8]

It was equally important to ensure accessibility to the law by insisting that all complaints and reports of crimes were properly investigated, even if considerable expense was incurred in doing so. People did not travel great distances to seek the aid of the authorities, Porter believed, unless they honestly considered themselves grossly wronged. Such a man was the coloured servant of a field cornet in the Roggeveld, five days distant from Worcester, who complained to Porter that his master assaulted him and his wife with a sjambok after a dispute over the grazing of sheep. Porter ordered inquiries to be made, because the future peace and well-being of the colony would be seriously affected if disputes between employer and employed were not investigated through a desire to spare the public purse.[9] Crimes beyond the frontier, in which colonial subjects were involved, merited the same sort of investigation. In 1861 he recommended the resident magistrate of Namaqualand to go in person to Bushmanland to ascertain the truth about reports of a massacre, for 'if it appears that very many miserable Bushmen have been slaughtered, and this for acts for which humane men would scarcely shoot their dogs, it behoves us, I conceive, to spare neither time nor money in discovering the facts and bringing the perpetrators to justice'.[10] Protection against exploitation was another of Porter's preoccupations. The apprenticeship of black children to white masters was a constant matter of concern to him. In an attempt to minimise abuses he laid down as a general rule that black youths from beyond the border should not be apprenticed to the person who brought them into the colony. Any other course, he feared, would tend to establish a slave trade on the borders, for, whether children were purchased to impose slavery or to confer freedom upon them would be a matter of complete indifference to the natives beyond the boundary who would be tempted, by fair means or foul, to procure the marketable article.[11] The welfare of the apprentice was the major consideration. A man called Swart, with whom a black girl took refuge from the man who brought her into the colony, was approved as a suitable master for her because she appeared to be attached to him and his family and because his only involvement in the case was 'by showing such kindness to a poor ill-used child as induced her to run away from a cruel master'.[12] Porter also stipulated safeguards for adults from beyond the frontier. He was not averse to the introduction of a few Zulu families from Natal in 1843 as an experiment, believing that they could not be forced to come since they would be travelling by ship. But they might be deluded and deceived. The officer commanding in Natal should, therefore, be instructed to examine, through an interpreter, every man about to be brought to the Cape, and the superintendent of police should see that they got a wage agreement and a maximum contract of a year when they arrived. It would be in the interest of all parties if one or more in each batch could understand some Dutch.[13]

Undue harshness on the part of the authorities towards blacks incurred Porter's wrath. After a member of the Cape Mounted Police had shot a black man trying to evade arrest for being in the colony without a pass, it emerged that the officer in command had given his force two instructions, that a call to stand was an actual arrest, and that a man called upon to stand who ran away was to be shot. Porter described these instructions as grossly and dangerously illegal. It was a matter, he said, for surprise, regret and immediate action on the part of the government.[14] He was equally outspoken when a detachment of the same force burnt the huts of some Mfengu and others near Uitenhage in March 1858. The resident magistrate, he felt, could not have left matters more to chance if he had been giving orders to remove some trespassing cattle, and his clerk and the town clerk were equally remiss. As for the sergeant in command of the police, he first proposed to prosecute him, but eventually decided that he had been acting under a mistaken sense of duty. Still, if he had not been dismissed already, he ought to be. The victims, 'the poor people who have been burned out, with almost all their means of living', had suffered a most outrageously illegal proceedings for which public officers were to blame and they should be compensated from public funds.[15]

Porter's concern for justice was not one-sided; unlike the philanthrophists, he showed no bias towards coloured and black people. It was never part of his philosophy that the black man could do no wrong. He did not hesitate to take action against coloured transgressors or to reprimand overzealous partisan missionaries. Within a few weeks of his arrival in the colony he was shocked by the brutality of a party of coloured men who massacred some San cattle thieves on the frontier. What struck him most forcibly was that they were men of good character who returned home 'with consciences as clear as if they had been out upon a hunting party for exterminating wolves and had met good success'. Knowing that he had no hope of securing a conviction he resolved to frighten them by having them arrested and imprisoned for some time before announcing his intention not to prosecute.[16] Again he was prepared to put on trial for robbery and murder a party of San and Coloureds from the Kat River who went on commando against the Thembu and shot numbers of them for no greater resistance than throwing one assegai and one stone. He also disapproved strongly of the Kat River missionaries' role in the affair: 'One at least of the Messrs Read permitted himself to be carried ... beyond the line of conduct which ought to characterise a minister of peace'.[17] He approved of stern measures against the Coloureds of the Kat River Settlement who 'so wickedly' rebelled in 1851, and he regarded the blacks who were involved in the frontier war of 1850-53, 'not as enemies, entitled to the rights of enemies, but, as in law, thieves and pirates'.[18] Native customs such as the more sinister aspects of witchcraft he tried to eradicate. Since there was no law to punish witchcraft as such, he suggested that acts which, under other circumstances, would be allowed to pass unpunished might be seized upon as a means of striking at offenders. On the other hand, he was reluctant to interfere with rainmakers. Extortioners they might be, but not necessarily conscious cheats.[19] The punishment of witchcraft murders presented a similar problem, for the perpetrators did not regard themselves as guilty of a crime. He favoured imprisonment and banishment, rather than death, for, as he commented in the case of a man who had offered five oxen as a fit compensation for a witchcraft killing, 'with men of conscience so miserably darkened one would not hang such a man if a better punishment could be made the means of enlightening him and deterring others'.[20]

Porter's conviction about the need for enlightenment and his reservations about primitive societies were confirmed by his first personal experience of life beyond the frontier when he accompanied the governor, Sir Peregrine Maitland, in May-June 1845 on a mission to revise the treaties which had been made with local chiefs in the troubled territory beyond the Orange river, where Boers, Griqua and Sotho were jockeying for position. He was unimpressed both by the men and the mode of life he encountered. Waterboer, the Griqua captain from Griquatown, disappointed him, after the encomium heaped upon him by Dr John Philip, the superintendent of the London Missionary Society; Porter thought him an insignificant little fellow, very overrated, and what he said had no relevance to anything. Adam Kok, the other Griqua captain, disgusted him by refusing to let the army use an unfinished house he was building at Phi-lippolis unless he was paid £3.10.0. a month, one of several in-stances 'illustrative of the high-mindedness and gratitude of the Griqua chief'. Hendrik Hendriks, the secretary to government at Philippolis, on the other hand, though dirty and ill-clad, deli-vered 'very fluently and well a long and really able speech', and Moshweshwe, the Sotho chief he considered the most intelligent of the black leaders, though 'awfully longwinded'. Adam Kok's missionary at Philippolis, Thomson, struck him as being a smart young man, not unconscious of his smartness, and by tempera-ment and position a good deal of a partisan. Porter admitted to treating him with more asperity than he had intended, after coming to the conclusion that Thomson was in correspondence with Fairbairn of the *South African Commerical Advertiser*. Some years later he expressed the opinion that the necessity of keep-ing Captain Kok and his missionary in due subjection was an object of such importance as to be second only to the great duty of doing right.

The first conference with the Griqua was held in Colesberg, in an inconveniently small room, but as the chiefs and their coun-sellors were kept in a through draught between the open door and the open windows the stench was less intolerable than it might have been. The governor's party then moved on to Philip-polis which consisted of a few houses of brick or clay, none with any appearance of cleanliness or comfort, a church standing across the main street, 'broken backed', partly unroofed and in a state of general decay, and numbers of 'wigwams', some six or seven feet in diameter and three or four feet high, made of mat-ting, with an opening, serving as chimney and door, through which the inhabitants crawled on all fours. Some of the houses had plots of land attached, apparently meant for gardens, but there was no sign of anything ever having been planted. Milk, butter, potatoes and any other sort of vegetables were unobtainable. A company of dragoons, encamped about a quarter of a mile up the stream which supplied the town with water, had constructed a dam to deepen the stream, but the Griqua had made no attempt to follow their example; women were still scooping the water out of the mud. There were, said Porter, cutty sarks enough among these women but Tam O'Shanter would not have had his 'een enriched' if he had been looking on. Indeed, when a fight broke out among them, he thought, 'in their smoked carosses, dirty skins, half human features and wild gestures they were like so many devils'. Huddled round some embers in the middle of their mat huts were families consisting of ten or twelve, the father in filthy tatters, the woman, skinny and emaciated 'with her disgusting dugs hanging down flabbily upon her knees', the elder children naked except for a scanty sheep-skin over the shoulders, the younger children quite naked. Amongst those he spoke to in Dutch he did not find much courtesy, but there was no incivility.

From Philippolis the party went to Touwfontein where, in the presence of a great number of chiefs and followers, the negotiations were carried on to the accompaniment of feasting and military displays. Porter found it impossible to get at the truth on any aspect of the situation. 'Great, huge, heavy lumbering lies, as rank as assvogels*, fly about as rapidly as swallows.... Beyond the Orange river at least, all men are liars', and his summing up of the whole Transorangian venture was that they were there 'on behalf of great principles and not of a great people'.[21]

Of course, a good deal of what Porter had to say about the peoples beyond the Orange had nothing to do with their colour; much of it was the normal reaction of a Victorian middle-class person to the lower orders of society. Porter's friend Lynar thought the poor 'Hottentots' of the Cape 'almost as ragged and

*vultures

103

wretched as the more destitute of our own countrymen' and he likened them to the Irish migrant labourers who crowded Eden Quay in Dublin at the approach of the English harvest, 'with the added beauty that a fit of jaundice gives'.[22] Whatever measure of disillusionment Porter may have suffered, however, it did nothing to destroy his faith, as a liberal, in the possibility of progressing to better things. A desire to promote self-improvement was characteristic of his rulings as attorney general. He would be sorry, he once said, 'to believe that blacks from beyond the border were tolerated only as hewers of wood and drawers of water to the colonists.' If a man who had been admitted to the colony to look for work as a labourer found some honest means of support which enabled him to live in some way more suited to his notions than being the bondsman of another, he saw nothing in the law to prevent him and everything in sound policy to encourage such a spirit of improvement.[23] Service to the community was also to be encouraged. Coloured prisoners who volunteered for service in the frontier wars should be allowed to go, and go as free men. That coloured servants who joined the native levies should be threatened with punishment for breach of contract was reprehensible: 'My gorge rises at it. This may be wrong but I cannot help it'. Some farmers who tried to enlist Porter's help in preventing their servants from joining the native levies were dryly informed that he would be sorry to find them doing anything calculated to subject themselves to the reproach of neither turning out themselves, nor allowing the Khoikhoi to turn out.[24] When some inhabitants of the Kat River Settlement complained to him about not being summoned to serve as jurymen, he replied at length to their 'manly and intelligent address', assuring them that there was 'no distinction whatever of race or nation, creed or colour' among the Queen's subjects and consequently a Khoikhoi who had the qualifications required by law had as good a right to serve as any Englishman in the colony. One qualification was the possession of a certain amount of property, as some guarantee of the intelligence, integrity and independence of the juryman. In a free country, 'where the road to advancement is alike open to all classes', such a provision could not be considered a grievance, 'and it certainly will not be so regarded by the inhabitants of Kat River, who are honourably elevating their social condition by a course of prosperous industry'. It was because of the other qualifiction, residence within six hours on horseback from the circuit town, that their services had not been called upon, and in this they were being treated equally with other colonists. 'With any other treatment', Porter concluded, 'I should be the first to admit that you should never rest content'.[25]

Porter adopted the same principle of equality of treatment when representative government was being planned for the colony. In the memorandum which he prepared at the governor's request in 1848 he affirmed his faith in a colour-blind franchise:

> I deem it to be just and expedient to place the suffrage within the reach of the more intelligent and industrious of the men of colour, because it is a privilege which they would prize and a privilege which they deserve, and because by showing to all classes, those above and those below them, that no man's station is, in this free country, determined by the accident of his colour, all ranks of men are stimulated to improve or maintain their relative positions.[26]

To ensure the inclusion of the coloured man he proposed to base the franchise on the 'almost nominal qualification' of ocupying a tenement valued at £25. When he was accused later of acting at the bidding of the secretary of state he retorted that the secretary of state could have known nothing about his proposal when he made it and that, indeed, it was the secretary of state who took the idea from him.[27] This assertion is confirmed by statements made in the house of commons in November 1852. According to Sir John Pakington, secretary of state for war and the colonies, his predecessor, Earl Grey, had felt unable to express any opinion on the appropriate franchise for a colony so remote as the Cape; he preferred to abide by the views of those on the spot

— the legislative council and, especially, the attorney general, 'a gentleman distinguished in the colony for his ability, long service to the crown and his professional attainments' (a tribute greeted with cries of 'Hear, hear'). Earl Grey, therefore, made a literal copy of Porter's paragraph respecting the franchise and incorporated it into his own draft ordinances. Sir Charles Wood, who had been chancellor of the exchequer at the time, agreed that Porter's franchise proposal was sent back by Grey to the Cape unaltered.

At first, Porter's official colleagues were in broad agreement with him but by the time the constitutional proposals came up for serious consideration his most powerful colleague, John Montagu, the secretary to the government, and most of the other members of the legislative council had changed their minds in the light of the 1850 Kat River rebellion, and considerable opposition was being voiced in the colony. Porter saw no reason to shift his position. He would rather, he said, meet the Khoikhoi at the hustings giving his vote than meet him in the kloof or the ravine with his gun upon his shoulder, desperate at being deprived of the protection of a franchise intended for his protection. The £25 franchise was a *sine qua non* with him. Rather than disappoint the expectations of the coloured people he would be prepared to tear the draft constitution to pieces. Far from looking forward to the prospect of plunder or predominance they were apprehensive of changes which they did not fully understand. They needed encouragement, not repression. There was no question of the coloured voters being able to return a sufficient number of representatives to endanger the rights of property, but the rights of the coloured man would be in danger of violation by a parliament chosen entirely by men of property. Then, adapting Matthew Prior:

'Be to his faults a little blind
   And to his virtues very kind
And clasp the padlock on his mind',

he concluded with a warning:

> If you do not secure the feelings, if you do not clasp the pad-
> lock on the mind, vain will be all your attempts by bolts and
> fetters of the other sort to keep tranquillity and order in a
> country where every man is a soldier and where the coloured
> man, feeling that he is denied what he deserves, concludes that
> he is first disfranchised in order that he may be afterwards
> oppressed.[28]

Porter's franchise was accepted by the colonial office and
remained unchanged for over thirty years. When Rhodes and
Hofmeyr were working for a higher franchise qualification in
the early 1890s they both alleged that Porter had had second
thoughts towards the end of his career, when the expansion of
the colony brought great numbers of black people within its
borders.[29] They did not substantiate their claim with precise
evidence. Though incidental criticism was levelled against the
franchise from time to time the only direct assault made on it
during Porter's residence at the Cape was in 1866 when a bill to
raise the property qualification from £25 to £50 received a
second reading but was subsequently dropped. Porter was not
in parliament when the bill was debated — it was in the interval
between his ex-officio membership and his election for Cape
Town — but there is nothing to suggest that he ever changed his
mind on the franchise, as he did on the desirability of a second
chamber in parliament. When an attempt was made in the
house of assembly in 1870 by a Grahamstown member to
require voters to pay a registration fee, ostensibly to avoid
abuses but primarily to restrict the number of coloured voters,
Porter voiced his decided opposition because, he said, it was for
the public good that the body to elect the members of the legislature should be as large as possible.[30]

A refusal to be discouraged or to be stampeded into precipi-
tate action characterised Porter's attitude to the non-white
peoples of the colony. The crisis of the early 1850s did not
undermine his faith in progress, though it forced him to reexa-

mine some of his ideas and to make a realistic appraisal of its significance. Since his arrival in the colony he had been involved in advising successive governors, after 1846 the governor as high commissioner as well, on the complex problems beyond the frontier arising from the Great Trek. He had always shown his desire to protect the non-white peoples from encroachment or destruction by the whites. What had alarmed him about the situation in Natal in 1844 was the threat of the emigrant Boers to expel the Zulus, a 'truly nefarious project' even admitting that the influx of Zulus had been too great.[31] The Maitland treaties with the Transorangian chiefs, which he had helped to frame, had been preferable to annexation of the territory because:

> By avoiding annexation an experiment will be tested which has never yet been tried, viz, whether the extinction of the coloured races before whites, usually ascribed to the civilisation of the latter, may not, with greater truth, be ascribed to their defective form of civilisation, and whether the contact of white with coloured, when the former are more highly civilised, may not merely consist with the safety but advance the political independence of the latter. This higher civilisation is certainly not in our Emigrants. But it may be held to be in the colonial government. Assisting the native tribes till they can go alone, it may if territory be not taken, leave them when they can go alone. But once advance your boundary in name to any extent and you must soon advance it in reality to the full extent and the result will be the old oil and water process and the natives will sink into servitude and the whites will by force, or otherwise, usurp the entire soil.[32]

It had been with regret at 'the reversal of what was so long a cherished and most noble policy' that he had accepted the expediency of withdrawing from the Orange River Sovereignty.[33]

The outbreak of another frontier war, and one for which, he held, the colonists were not to blame, led him to conclude that the blacks beyond the frontier must be completely subjugated. In principle, still, he would have preferred them to be completely independent, and to have relations between them and

108

the colonists regulated by treaty. That arrangement had been shown not to work, however. Nor had the system of partial independence. If subjugation did not work, he saw nothing for it but something he feared to think of, the acceptance of the doctrine, advanced by the Sheffield M.P., J. A. Roebuck, in the house of commons, that the coloured races were incapable of being civilised and must be rooted out. If it came to that, 'darkness, thick darkness, rests upon the future'. The rebellion of the Kat River Khoikhoi he attributed, not to any ill-treatment, but to a variety of causes. One was a 'foolish notion of nationality', inspired by the belief that they were the ancient owners of the land of which the white man had dispossessed them. Another was envy, when they contrasted their own squalid poverty with the prosperity of the whites and attributed it to the greed of the whites and not to their own 'sloth and inactivity'. Ignorance, in spite of the money and the missionary zeal expended on them, was partly responsible, because it led them to panic and rebel when irritated colonists talked of vagrancy laws which the proposed parliament would enact. A feeling among the Khoikhoi that they had been called upon to do more than their share in the war of 1846 played a part in driving some of them into rebellion. The indiscreet zeal of certain missionaries also contributed. There was, Porter said, no nobler gospel in the entire Bible than that 'God hath made of one blood all the nations that dwell upon the face of the earth', but it was a gospel which required to be preached with soberness and some degree of caution, 'lest the ignorant and unstable among them should wrest it, as they do all other scripture, to their own destruction'.[34] Events which moved Porter to reflect along these lines clearly represented a setback to the ideals he had in mind. Yet he did not allow them to deflect him from his course. The rebellion of the Kat River Khoikhoi was no reason for denying the vote to all coloured men, he contended; as well disfranchise the Boers of Graaff Reinet because of the Slachter's Nek rebellion of 1815. He even drew some encouragement from the rebellion. The Khoikhois' notion of being a nation, their claim to original ownership of the land, the recognition of the principle of hereditary right were bad as leading to rebellion but good as giving an indication of social progress, a progress which might, in the future, continue to go forward. A hundred years before, the Khoikhoi had had no more idea of nationality than the baboons, and as little notion of rights and privileges.[35]

Porter was equally restrained in his reaction to new problems beyond the frontier. Papers submitted to him on Moshweshwe's possible connections with the Xhosa cattle-killings in 1857 suggested to him that the cattle-killing was 'the dream of a people who had lost confidence in themselves rather than as the means by which such a people as kaffirs would prepare for war'. Whatever the nature of the event, Moshweshwe had no connection with it, he concluded. Those who suspected him of a design to combine the tribes for his own purpose were crediting him with greater subtlety than Porter was prepared to ascribe to him, much as he respected his ability. But, in the circumstances, reports that Moshweshwe was a believer, was in communication with Kreli, (the whites' name for Sarhili), was killing hard, was receiving the first fruits of the new cattle and the first visits of the new people were certain to be in general circulation.[36] He had reservations, too, about the governor's court actions against other chiefs involved in the cattle-killing, contending in the case of Mhala that if there was reason to believe he was a threat to the peace of the country it would have been better to proceed against him under martial law than to convict him 'under a defective situation, supported by what strikes me as somewhat defective evidence'.[37]

Basic to all that Porter said and did during his thirty-four years at the Cape was his aversion to anything that savoured of oppression. He had publicly declared his hatred of oppression in the early days and that remained his guiding principle to the end. One of his last public duties was to serve on the federation commission of 1872. All his questions were designed to elicit opinions on the possibility of discrimination against non-white servants by a provincial legislature, and in a blueprint prepared for the commission he stipulated that the provincial legislature, if it came into being, should be forbidden to make any distinction of race or colour when regulating the rights and duties of servants and masters.[38]

1   *GTJ*, 24 January 1852, CA, AG 2158.
2   LB, 1853-5, pp.189-90, CA, AG 2160; Speeches, pp.57-8.
3   *Further papers re representative assembly*, H.C. 1851, xxxvii [1362] 1, p.168.
4   *GTJ*, 20 October 1840.
5   Porter to Lynar, 20 June 1845, SAL Porter papers; *Correspondence re Kafir tribes*, H.C. 1847, xxxviii [786], pp.18-19.
6   LB, 1853-5, p.147-8, CA, AG 2160.
7   Rpts, 1857-9, p.489, CA, AG 2622.
8   Ibid., p.493.
9   LB, 1853-5, pp.199-200, CA, AG 2160; LB, 1855-7, pp.34-5, AG 2161.
10   LB, 1861-4, p.66, CA, AG 2164.
11   Rpts, 1838-41, p.231, CA, AG 2615; Rpts, 1841-3, p.228, AG 2616; LB, 1830-47, p.379, AG 2157.
12   LB, 1846-50, p.120, CA, AG 2618.
13   Rpts, 1840-6, pp.3-5, CA, AG 2617.
14   Rpts, 1857-9, pp.408-9, CA, AG 2622.
15   Ibid,. pp.474, 523.
16   Journal, SAL, Porter papers.
17   Rpts, 1843-6, pp.34-6, CA, AG 2617.
18   Rpts, 1853-4, pp.151-4, CA, AG 2620; LB, 1853-5, p.307, AG 2160.
19   LB, 1855-8, p.62, CA, AG 2161; A. E. du Toit, 'The Cape frontier... 1847-66', in *AYB*, 1954, i. 148.
20   LB, 1847-51, p.245, CA, AG 2158.
21   Porter to Lynar, 15 June, 24 June, 28 June, 5 July 1845, SAL Porter papers; J. F. Midgley, 'The Orange River Sovereignty (1848-54)', in *AYB*, 1949. ii. 261.
22   Lynar to Frank Porter, 13 October 1840, SAL, Porter papers.
23   LB, 1830-47, pp.148-9, CA, AG 2157.
24   Rpts, 1843-6, p.292, CA, AG 2617; LB, 1847-51, p.519, AG 2158; *Cape Monitor*, 31 January 1851.
25   LB, 1830-47, pp.103-4, CA, AG 2157.
26   *Establishment of representative assembly*, H. C. 1850, xxxviii [1337] 2, p.8.
27   *GTJ*, 3 April 1852.

28 *Further papers re assembly*, H.C. 1852-3, lxvi [1581] 1, pp.217-21; *GTJ*, 3 April 1852; ibid. 22 January 1853.

29 *Assembly debates*, 1891, pp.327-8; 1892, p.151.

30 *GTJ*, 5 March 1870.

31 Rpts, 1843-6, pp.173-7, CA, AG 2617.

32 Porter to Lynar, 15 June 1845, SAL, Porter papers.

33 J. F. Midgley, op. cit. ii. 454-6.

34 *GTJ*, 13 December 1851.

35 Ibid., 3 April 1852.

36 Rpts, 1857-9, pp.38-40, CA, AG 2622.

37 J. B. Peires, *The dead will arise*, pp.231, 236.

38 *Report on federation* [G. 9-72], pp.64, 80, 100-1, 145, lxxvii.

Above: Colesberg, where Porter had 'the privilege of being fed upon by bugs and flees'.

Bottom: Philippolis, Adam Kok's headquarters. 'The first impression as you enter Philippolis is not imposing'.

Top right: The first opening ceremony of the Cape parliament at Government House, Cape Town on 16 September 1854.

Bottom right: The banqueting hall of the Goede Hoop Masonic Lodge was the meeting place of the House of Assembly from 1854 until 1884.

Cradock Kloof Pass, the old pass over the Outenique Mountains between the Long Kloof and George. 'All I had ever heard or read of this infernal road proved nothing to the horrible reality'.

Anti-convict public meeting at the Commercial Exchange, Cape Town on 4 July 1849.

Opening ceremony of the Cape parliament at the Shaw Hall,
Grahamstown on 28 April 1864.

9

Porter In Cape Politics

Porter was a legal officer, not a political one, but the duties of a colonial attorney general were such that the line between the two spheres was sometimes blurred. The wide scope of the office was emphasised by the secretary of state for the colonies, Sir Edward Bulwer-Lytton, in a letter to the governor of Hongkong in 1858. The special function of a colonial attorney general, he said, was to give counsel and assistance to the local government. It was not enough for him merely to perform his formal duties by doing the legal business incumbent on him.

> His functions are much more extensive, more important, and more delicate than these. The local government must have the benefit of his general assistance in the many points on which a lawyer's counsel is constantly required.[1]

Porter's assistance was sought on the legal aspect of political issues in his capacity as legal adviser to the government, but he was also *ex officio* a member of the executive council and of the legislative council and as such he was directly involved in politics. Porter, indeed, claimed that he and the other office-holders were 'perhaps more involved in politics than any other men in the country'.[2]

The day after he arrived in the colony Porter was sworn in as an executive counsellor:

> I abjured the Pretender, as I had done when called to the bar, and declared my belief that there was not any transubstantiation in the elements of bread and wine at the Lord's Supper. How nonsensical is all this.

After the ceremony was over he was plunged straightaway into colonial problems; the governor talked to him about the native treaties, 'Which appeared to him to be susceptible of improvement', and about the frontier colonists' complaints of wholesale cattle stealing and their hankering after the old commando system. A week later he attended his first legislative council meeting. There he resolved a problem he found awaiting him with the tact that so largely accounts for the favourable impression he made at the Cape from the beginning. The council was considering a master and servant bill necessitated by the ending of slavery. His predecessor, Oliphant, had characteristically left the preparation of the draft to Mr Justice Menzies, but the judge's bill was unacceptable, mainly because it recognised colour as a distinction among the labouring population. Musgrave, acting attorney general, had thereupon produced another version which stimulated Menzies, who was 'very slow to believe that Musgrave or any other man alive could do anything as well as he himself', to frame the elaborate bill which was then before the council. People expected Porter to withdraw this bill and bring in one of his own, but he decided that it would be foolish for a newcomer to discard a bill drafted by the touchy Menzies, and one, besides, on a very sensitive subject. Accordingly, he expressed his approval of the bill but reserved the right to amend it on details where necessary.

By his expeditious action on another problem inherited from his predecessor, Porter ingratiated himself with the leading citizens of Cape Town. An ordinance establishing municipal institutions in Cape Town, passed by the legislative council before he arrived, had proved to be unworkable. Some of the regulations were 'exquisitely Pickwickian' and amused him 'by their solemn folly'. It was a 'beautifully bungled piece of legislation' which would have to be replaced by a new measure. Since he regarded municipal institutions as a 'proper extension of the principles of rational liberty' he set to work on a revision immediately and the outcome was that Cape Town got its municipality in 1840.

Porter had been in the colony just over a month when a challenging situation arose in the legislative council. Opinion in Cape Town was sharply divided over a bills of exchange bill which one of the unofficial members, Ebden, had introduced. The governor was strongly opposed to it, and in the course of a debate he called upon Porter, as his law adviser, to support him. 'I felt that now or never was the time for firmness and temper', was Porter's reaction. He rose immediately and in courteous but unambiguous terms made his position clear. He was the governor's legal adviser, he said, not the governor his. All attempts to control his legislative freedom on a question of this nature would encounter his unyielding resistance. If he found that his office precluded him from speaking and voting as he saw fit he would look out for the first ship leaving Table Bay. He concluded his declaration with the lines:

> Thy spirit, Independence, let me share,
>   Lord of the lion-heart, and eagle eye.

The episode caused a great sensation. The council chamber and the passages were crowded with spectators and even those who supported the governor's stand on the bill were warm in their approval of Porter's response. The newspapers in Cape Town had already commented favourably on his performance in the legislative council and they enthusiastically applauded his spirited assertion of independence.[3]

Within a few weeks of his arrival Porter had revealed the manner and spirit in which he proposed to discharge his duties. Those duties were manifold and all-embracing. Apart from his work as public prosecutor any aspect of Cape politics or administration could be referred to him in his advisory capacity. Governors consulted him, formally and informally, about whatever problems they had in hand, and after 1846 they called upon him for advice in their role as high commissioner also, sometimes by direction of the colonial office. Dispatches of secretaries of state on major issues of imperial policy were submitted to him for his opinion and the minutiae of parish pump politics equally came his way.

After his early involvement in the problems of Transorangia his advice was sought on the subsequent setting up of the Orange River Sovereignty and its abandonment; he was much concerned with the extension of British rule to Natal following on its annexation; he was asked to give an opinion on problems arising from the frontier wars, the Kat River rebellion and the cattle killing; and he was consulted about the establishment of British Kaffraria and the introduction of German settlers.

His function was to advise, particularly on legal implications; what happened thereafter was for others to decide. The extent of his influence in this sphere is difficult to assess, for he was not the governor's only adviser, but he was on good terms with all the governors of his day except Wodehouse and well thought of by them; his high standing with the colonial office was vouched for by several colonial secretaries and, more significantly, by Herman Merivale, the permanent under-secretary, and his long tenure of the attorney generalship which gave him an unrivalled knowledge of the colony and of public affairs placed him at an advantage over other office holders at the Cape.

It was in the legislative sphere, however, that Porter made his most individual and characteristic contribution. Not only did he draft government ordinances but he also took a leading part in the actual legislative process where his grasp of parliamentary procedure, his skill in debate and his strong personality made him a commanding figure. On the major issues of colonial politics he expressed his views, uninhibited by his official position and guided always by his liberal principles.

One of his earliest interventions in the legislative council was on the question of immigration, a matter of pressing concern to many colonists at the time because of the dislocation in the labour market caused by the abolition of slavery and the end of the apprenticeship arrangement. Though as an Irishman he was well disposed towards relieving distress in the British Isles, he

116

doubted if any British scheme of assisted emigration was likely to benefit the Cape Colony because the flow of emigration was to Canada and Australia. Edward Gibbon Wakefield's scheme was quite inapplicable to the Cape where there was no waste land worth mentioning to sell. In any case he questioned the soundness of the scheme in general; it was not, he thought, by taking from the first settlers a great deal of whatever capital they had, and checking the tendency to spread, that America had become great. As for the Cape's own limited resources, they would be better used in developing roads than in financing immigration. Besides, the colony had a labouring population already, a coloured population, and in spite of the talk of stupidity and sloth he believed in the potential of the coloured labourers if masters would exert themselves. To import European labourers in large numbers in this situation could well result in 'the additional inflation of the white and in the additional degradation of the black'. There could be a risk:

of nourishing a feeling of caste even in the very working class — of creating an aristocracy of the foulest and most disgusting of all imaginable aristocracies — the wretched aristocracy of skin.[4]

To a proposal in 1842 that a group of juvenile criminals should be sent to the Cape, Porter was vehemently opposed. Not only did he speak against it in the legislative council but he seconded the resolution at a public political meeting in Cape Town, claiming that in spite of his official position there was no impropriety 'in taking a position which I am always glad to occupy — that of meeting, as a citizen, the rest of my fellow-citizens, in order to deliberate upon any matter vitally affecting the public welfare'. He summed up his attitude by declaring that he was disposed to write up in very large letters for the benefit of the home government the words, 'Commit no nuisance here'.[5] His sentiments had not changed when the colonial secretary sent a ship load of ticket-of-leave men to the Cape in 1849. His sympathies at first were with the protest movement which sprang up in Cape Town but he incurred unpopularity by ruling that the governor could not send the ship away, though he might retain the convicts on board pending further instructions. As the Anti-Convict Association became more violent in its opposition he condemned its excesses but advised against declaring it an illegal body. Later he described it as a movement 'most noble in its origins but discreditable towards its close, for it degenerated into a wanton persecution and organised attempt to overawe the government'.[6]

The Anti-Convict Association's hostility to the government was not motivated only by opposition to the dumping of convicts on the colony; it was an expression of dissatisfaction with the system of government as well. From time to time since the 1820s petitions had been drawn up asking for a representative assembly in line with other British colonies. The legislative council which was established in 1834 was regarded as a poor substitute and its popularity did not increase with the years. As Porter said, few competent men could be found to serve on it. Those who did were taunted with being creatures of the government and consequently, in an effort to show their independence, they tended to be 'blown about by every wind of doctrine out of doors'.[7] Lord Durham's report on Canada in 1839 stimulated interest in constitutional reform and the setting up of municipal councils was hailed as a step in the right direction. One Cape Town newspaper saw in them 'the seeds of that entire self-government with respect to all internal affairs which the imperial government must now concede with the least poss-ible delay'.[8] Two petitions from Cape Town in 1841 were forwarded by the governor to the secretary of state, Lord Stanley, with a supporting letter but the imperial government still hesitated to concede a local assembly. Lord Stanley foresaw great practical difficulties in a colony so sparsely populated and so extensive, he feared oppression of the coloured peoples, and he was conscious of divided opinion at the Cape where the pressure for a new constitution came from Cape Town while the Eastern Province was not prepared to join in the demand unless it was given a separate government or unless the seat of government was fixed at a more central place than Cape Town. It was only after the outbreak of another expensive frontier war that a new colonial secretary, Earl Grey, reopened the question in November 1846 by asking the governor for his comments on Lord Stanley's dispatch of 1842.[9] In response to this request Governor Sir Harry Smith consulted with Porter, 'a man in whose judgement I have great confidence', and directed him to frame a memorandum. The Cape parliament which eventually emerged was primarily Porter's creation. 'He was substantially (under Lord Grey's direction) the framer of the present Cape constitution', wrote Herman Merivale some years later, 'and it was a task of no common difficulty'.[10]

Porter came down firmly on the side of unity. His memorandum of 17 March 1848 proposed the establishment of one parliament for the whole colony, meeting in Cape Town, and consisting of a nominated upper house and an elected lower house. Members should be required to satisfy a moderate property qualification but the franchise qualification should be low because 'perhaps there is no country in the world where mere differences of rank or class, complexion being the same, is less marked than it is at the Cape of Good Hope, especially in the country districts', and also because justice and expediency demanded that the more intelligent and industrious of the coloured population should be included in the electorate. The existing legislative council having fallen into disrepute, no time should be lost in establishing the new constitution. Recalling the effects of delaying Catholic emancipation in Ireland he added, 'all reason and all experience show that those rulers give twice who give quickly and that no privileges are so sure to be abused as privileges wrung from reluctant hands'.[11]

The governor submitted Porter's memorandum to the other

members of the executive council and to the judges, and when they all expressed themselves in favour of representative government he asked Porter to frame a draft order in council setting out a scheme for a parliament. The new document, which embodied all the essential proposals of the original one, was completed in June 1848 and dispatched to London. By the time it had been considered and amended, mainly by the substitution of an elective for a nominated upper house, the anti-convict agitation at the Cape had dislocated the legislative council which, in accordance with the instructions contained in letters patent issued in May 1850, was to enact a constitution ordinance. The governor reconstituted the council but four of the new unofficial members resigned after acrimonious debates in which Porter shouldered the major burden. The situation was further complicated at the end of 1850 by the outbreak of war on the eastern frontier and the rebellion of the Kat River Khoikhoi. These events had the two-fold effect of leading a good many people in the colony to have second thoughts about the low franchise and to look more favourably on the Eastern Province's claim for a separate government, and of convincing the colonial office that the introduction of a new constititution must be postponed. Porter, in a minute of 15 January 1851, maintained that the longer the establishment of a parliament was put off 'the more must be increased and irritated those jealousies of race and class which all good men desire to obliterate'. He also stoutly defended a franchise which would shut out nothing 'but vagrancy and crime'.[12] With the appointment of four new unofficial members the legislative council was able to reassemble in October 1851. In the same month draft ordinances were received from the imperial government for submission to the legislative council.

The debates in the legislative council centred very largely on the £25 franchise, with some members in favour of postponing discussion of the constitution altogether until the frontier war was over. Porter defended the £25 franchise in speech after speech. He accepted responsibility for it, saying that it originated with him and not with the colonial office. He admitted that the coloured man might be the prey of political adventurers but so would others. 'I have formed', he said, 'but a low estimate of the discrimination of the mass of people in regard to the choice of their favourites. Men must often receive franchises before they are fit to use them. You must let them into the water before they can swim. Both Boers and Hottentots have much to learn'. He did not believe that in any constituency coloureds could defeat the whites. But even if they could, he would not give up the £25 franchise, for 'the coloured classes should, like every other class, have their appropriate safety-valve, because when there is no provision for letting off steam the boiler bursts'. He scoffed at the idea that the coloured vote would threaten the rights of property, but without it the rights of labour would be endangered. He contended that the Kat River rebellion was no justification for denying the franchise to the coloured man. But most of all he reiterated the argument of his original memorandum that justice and expediency demanded the opening of the franchise to the coloured man. To those of his critics who said that the colony was not ripe for responsible government he replied 'No people ever ripen till the sun of freedom has begun to shine on them'. In spite of his efforts, however, the constitution ordinance was passed in March 1852 with two major amendments, the franchise qualification was raised and the property qualification for members of the upper house was doubled. Porter and two of his colleagues, the auditor general and the collector of customs, recorded their dissent from the amendments to the franchise, declaring that this would 'produce a dangerous degree of distrust and alarm'.[13] In the event, however, he carried the day for the orders in council ratifying the ordinances restored the £25 franchise.

Under the new constitution the attorney general was one of the office holders entitled to sit and speak but not to vote in both the legislative council and the house of assembly. As in the old legislative council Porter was a key figure, particularly in the house of assembly where he was allowed greater freedom of action. He was in a special position with regard to legislation. Governors referred to him matters which might conflict with existing laws. He had to decide whether something could be accomplished by government notice or proclamation or whether legislation was necessary and whether the prior consent of the imperial authorities was needed. He drafted government bills and proclamations and even bills originating from private members and public bodies. His knowledge of parliamentary procedure enabled him to guide and advise the inexperienced legislature and his skill in debate made him one of the most effective members of the parliament. He was so well-read and well-informed that he was never at a loss for the apt quotation or the relevant illustration. His ready wit could disarm an opponent, as when he told a member who was quoting statistics that nothing was so deceptive as statistics except faces. He could defuse an emotionally-charged debate by poking gentle fun at an argument, as when he reminded a member who was denouncing native dances which left servants unfit for work next day that young ladies also were sleepy after balls. He recalled members to a sense of realism, as when in a discussion on whether civil servants on probation could be summarily dismissed, he told them that in former times delinquent nuns had never been executed, that had been too harsh a term, but a niche had been built in a wall and they had been immured in it after being told:

Sister, let thy sorrows cease
Sinful sister, part in peace.

'Rhubarb is rhubarb, call it what you may, as Dr Slop said'. His formal speeches, often of two hours duration or more, were elaborately constructed, logical, lucid and eloquent and delivered with consumate skill. Even his bitterest opponents admitted his mastery of words: his 'monstrous notions' which 'drop like dew from the honeysuckle', his words, 'which he strings beautifully together so as to throw a magic charm over his audience'.[14]

The establishment of a parliament in 1854 marked a step towards the attainment of the self-governing status already enjoyed by the other large British colonies of settlement but the peculiar problems which had retarded the granting of representative government still militated against an easy transition to responsible government. One of the obstacles in the way was Eastern Province separatism which arose partly from the desire for greater security on the frontier, partly from conflicting economic interests between east and west and partly from anti-Dutch and anti-Cape Town feeling. Porter was strongly opposed to the easterners' demands. He had devised a constitution for the whole colony and he stood by it consistently when the easterners pressed their claims. He described separatism in 1859 as a movement inspired by the 1820 settlers of Grahamstown and, much as he admired the settlers, he reminded them that they did not constitute the colony, nor even the Eastern Province, but, he added caustically, unionist though he was in the Irish context, he would not oppose the repeal of the union between the colony and Grahamstown, if Grahamstown desired it. To remove the seat of government would reduce Cape Town to the level of Colesberg and a duplicate establishment would involve wasteful expense which could only be justified if a separate government was necessary, and he did not believe that it was, to protect life and property.[15] When parliament met in Grahamstown in 1864 he again affirmed his desire to see the colony remain one and undivided. The balance of races within the colony and the power and prestige of the colony beyond its borders would be imperilled by separation. 'Union is strength, or as the Dutch perhaps more strongly express it, Eendrag maak magt'. Nor was he in favour of the removal of the seat of government. The old capital of the colony had claims which it would be gross injustice to overlook. If he had to choose between the removal of the seat of government and separatism he would, 'not without sorrow and anxiety', take separation.[16]

Nevertheless, Porter was sympathetic to the grievances of the easterners, particularly to their troubles on the frontier, and he was responsible for a major judicial reform designed to alleviate one aspect of the frontier problem, the endemic theft of livestock, and thereby to ease the pressure for separation. The measure had a long history. When Porter returned from his journey to the frontier with Sir Peregrine Maitland in 1845 he found that Montagu, the secretary to the government, had drawn up a proposal to break up the supreme court and divide the colony into five judicial circles with one judge in each, the five judges to be assembled once a year to hear appeals. Porter opposed these sweeping changes with all his might; he was against destroying the supreme court as a court of first instance, against isolating the judges, against the danger of conflicting decisions, against the destruction of the bar. In spite of his efforts, the legislative council approved the scheme but the colonial secretary in London rejected it. Ten years later, by direction of the governor, he framed a bill giving a court of two judges to the Eastern Province. It passed the legislative council but was rejected by the house of assembly. Another proposal to establish three judicial circles, west, north and east, with three judges in the west and one in each of the other two was introduced by a member of the assembly in 1859 but it also fell through. In the Grahamstown parliament in 1864 Porter piloted through a bill, and, when it was rejected, another bill to establish a supreme court for the eastern frontier, for what was needed, he contended, was 'to diminish by some six or seven hundred miles the distance between some main and constant fountain of justice and a large proportion of our population whose position is trying, placed as they are in the midst of natives whose golden maxim would seem to be that stolen mutton is sweet'. The new court he believed would go far towards satisfying the

124

separatists; 'the best chance to keep the colony one is to make its supreme court two'.[17]

By keeping the colony one, Porter realised that it would more easily attain the goal of responsible government. As a member of an official executive working in an elected parliament he found his position difficult and irksome, particularly in the legislative council where he was in the humiliating position of not being allowed to move a motion. After long deliberation he came to the conclusion that the colony was ripe for the change, and, as always, he did not allow his official position to prevent him from expressing his opinion. When J. C. Molteno proposed in 1860 that the members of the executive council should be eligible for election to parliament Porter supported him, for there was 'no safety in stopping short of that point to which all reason and experience led — responsible government'.[18]

The only other member of the executive council who took the same stand was R. W. Rawson, the colonial secretary. At the beginning of 1862 Porter went on leave for a year. He returned to find a new governor, Sir Philip Wodehouse, who was convinced that responsible government could not function in the colony and who regarded Porter as 'by no means a source of strength to the government'.[19] When Rawson was appointed governor of the Bahamas, not long after, Porter was left as the only member of the executive council in favour of responsible government, an uncomfortable position from which he escaped by resigning from the attorney generalship on reaching the age of 60 in 1865. Pressure was immediately put on him to seek election to the house of assembly but it was not until 1869 that he agreed to stand for Cape Town and was elected at the head of the poll.

As a private member Porter was fully involved with his 'responsible' colleagues in the closing stages of their struggle with Wodehouse, and it was to him that the new governor, Sir Henry Barkly, turned when Attorney General Griffith refused to draft a constitution amendment bill after Molteno had at last got a motion in favour of responsible government through the house of assembly in 1871.[20] In the debate on the bill which he prepared Porter discounted any idea that responsible government would work wonders, though he was still as strongly in favour of the system as he had been more than ten years before when he had first come out in support of it. What he did expect was an infusion of fresh vigour and fresh energy into the body politic, a forward move on the path of progress. He wanted to see a strong executive, a career open to colonial talent and the character of parliament raised by making service in it the honourable road to high political office.[21] When the bill was re-introduced as a government measure and passed in 1872 it fell to the governor to implement it. Immediately the bill was through the two houses he sent for Porter to discuss how and when it should be brought into operation. Between June and October he had repeated consultations and correspondence with Porter about the selection of a prime minister and the composition of a ministry. At their first meeting on June 15 he offered Porter the post but he declined it, suggesting instead Molteno or Solomon. In October Barkly again appealed to him to head, or at least to join, a ministry. Porter categorically refused in terms which made it impossible, as Barkly said, to press him further. But he did promise, probably with Molteno in mind, that for the short time he was likely to remain in parliament he would support men 'who mean well and display average administrative ability and a fair amount of zeal and industry'. This support out of office would prove more useful, he thought, than anything he could do as a minister.[22]

What he was proposing, in effect, was to continue in the role of guide, philosopher and friend in which he had cast himself since his election to the house of assembly, though, as his participation in the responsible government controversy shows, that role was consistent with the advocacy of causes on which he held strong views. In the 1869 session, for example, he took up Saul Solomon's crusade on behalf of the voluntary principle, the withdrawal of state grants to various religious denominations, and in a two-hour speech pleaded eloquently for the ending of a system which was 'one mass of confusion and injustice, which taxed all to pay a few denominations and paid them on no intelligible principle'.[23] In the next session he introduced a bill to abolish capital punishment, with the object of submitting thoughts and arguments to the consideration of the house and the country, which, he believed, would bear fruit in due time.[24] In a debate on native affairs he expressed the opinion that the native policy of the colony was a domestic issue which was no concern of the imperial government and that the office of high commissioner could well be dispensed with, indeed, that it had only been created to enable Sir Henry Pottinger to provide for a protégé by appointing him as secretary.[25] It was not to such controversial matters, however, that Porter devoted his main attention. He took a major part in the work of parliament. He regularly introduced bills himself; he told the house when he was not satisfied with the construction of a bill; he offered to re-draft bills to make them work; and he frequently moved amendments. He guided the house in other matters too; for example, he moved the election of the speaker, he proposed that the governor's expenses in entertaining the Grand Duke Alexis of Russia should be borne by parliament, and he expounded the principles of responsible government to the house and prepared a memorandum for the guidance of ministers on the circumstances in which they should feel themselves obliged to resign.[26] A leader in the *Grahamstown Journal* summed up very well the position Porter occupied in Cape politics in his last years. 'He is taking a lion's share of the duties of the house. It is he who mends all the bills and carries all the measures. His great powers and his long practice in parliament give him an advantage which he will maintain as long as he is well enough for public life'.[27]

1   J. W. Norton-Kyshe, *Colonial attorneys general*, p.13.

2   *GTJ*, 29 May 1860.
3   Journal, SAL, Porter papers; *Speeches*, pp.vii-viii, 38. Porter was quoting from Tobias Smollett's *Ode to Independence*,
4   *Speeches*, pp.xli-xliv, 51-72.
5   Ibid., pp.104-19.
6   *GTJ*, 28 February 1852.
7   *Reception of convicts at Cape*, H. C. 1850, XXXVIII [1138] 223, p.11.
8   *SACA*, 8, 15 May 1839.
9   Grey to Pottinger, 22 November 1846, PRO, CO 48/264.
10   Minute, 8 November 1855, PRO, CO 48/371/458.
11   *Establishment of representative assembly at Cape*, H.C., 1850, XXXVIII [1137] 3, pp.4-11.
12   *Further papers re assembly*, H.C., 1851, XXXVII [1362] 1, pp.20-87, 166-8.
13   *Further papers re assembly*, H.C., 1852-3, LXVI [1581] 1, pp.281-2, 218-21; *GTJ*, 28 February, 3 April, 24 April, 1 May 1852; *Cape Monitor*, 24 March 1852.
14   *GTJ*, 28 February, 10 April, 20 May 1864, 7 July 1871.
15   Ibid., 30 April, 3 May 1859.
16   Ibid., 11 June 1864.
17   Ibid., 11 June, 14 June 1864.
18   Ibid., 29 May 1860.
19   Wodehouse to Edward Cardwell, 18 May 1864, COL, A3C15, Private correspondence of Wodehouse.
20   *Cape correspondence*, 1867-71, H.C., 1871, XLV [C459], 11, p.187.
21   *GTJ*, 10 July 1871.
22   Barkly to Porter, 12 June, 14 October, 17 October, 21 October 1871; Porter to Barkly, 14 June, 19 June, 18 October 1872; Barkly memo of conversation with Porter, 5 August 1872, SAL, MS 552, ff.18a-32, Molteno papers.
23   *GTJ*, 30 August 1869.
24   Ibid., 9 March 1870.
25   Ibid., 9 May 1873.
26   Ibid., 6 September 1869, 17 May, 12 July, 15 July, 22 July 1872, 9 May 1873; Cory Library, Rhodes University, MS 10,069, Sprigg papers.
27   *GTJ*, 8 May 1872.

PART III

Epilogue

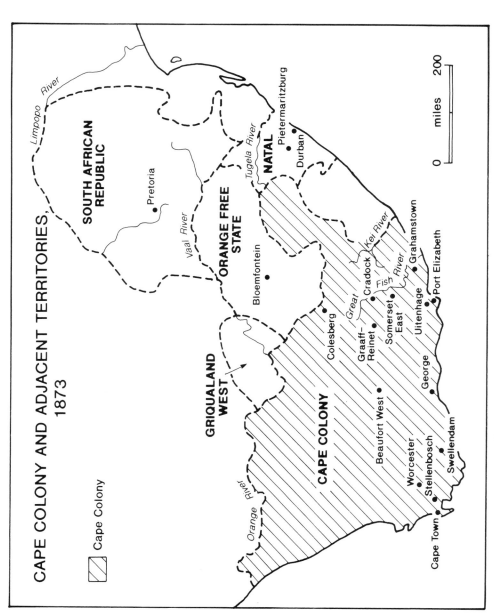

CAPE COLONY AND ADJACENT TERRITORIES, 1873

Cape Colony

SOUTH AFRICAN REPUBLIC

Limpopo River

Pretoria

Vaal River

ORANGE FREE STATE

Bloemfontein

GRIQUALAND WEST

Orange River

CAPE COLONY

Tugela River

NATAL

Pietermaritzburg

Durban

Colesberg

Graaff-Reinet

Great Fish River

Cradock

Kei River

Somerset East

Grahamstown

Uitenhage

Port Elizabeth

Beaufort West

George

Worcester

Stellenbosch

Swellendam

Cape Town

0   miles   200

Cape Colony and adjacent territories, 1873

130

10
Estimation

For the last seven years of his life Porter lived with his brother John Scott Porter in Belfast, first at 16 College Square East near the centre of the town and then at Lennoxvale on the outskirts. He took no part in public life in Ireland. He was a familiar figure in the Belfast Commercial Newsroom and he continued, as he had done all his life, to support charitable activities generously. Most of his time was taken up with family affairs, with an occasional holiday in Donegal or visit to London. He maintained a lively interest in the colony, corresponding with his niece, Frank's daughter Mary Eliza, who was in England, about Cape affairs, looking forward to news from Cape Town, and writing to his friends there. When the convocation of the University of the Cape of Good Hope elected him as the first chancellor in 1876 he was much gratified. A man with a reputation in literature or science and with social influence and standing would have been a more suitable choice, he felt, but:

> if, indeed no qualification were needed for the office to which I have been elected but a love of learning, and a desire to promote it, I should not deem myself entirely unfit. I have, as every one knows, no other qualifications. But if our gratitude for favours should be all the greater because we cannot but be sensible how little we have deserved them, the members of convocation who have followed an old colonial servant into his retirement in order to do him an honour of which any man might be justly proud, may rest assured that their generosity of feeling is justly estimated and will never be forgotten.[1]

If proof is needed of his continued attachment to the colony it is to be found in the terms of his will. He bequeathed well over a third of his fortune to public purposes at the Cape. After providing for a large number of friends and relatives, amongst them 46 women, by bequests ranging from £5,000 each to two of his brothers, to £25 each for his brother's servants, and in this way disposing of something in excess of £35,550, he left £20,000 for the establishment of a reformatory for boys at the Cape. His friend Hugh Lynar, he said, had often lamented the lack of such an institution. Should the Cape parliament, for any reason, decide against the establishment of a reformatory he asked that the money might be used for some other public purpose and expressed the wish that a portion of it should be applied to promoting the higher education of women through the agency of the University of the Cape of Good Hope. He then bequeathed £250 to the South African Public Library; £100 each to the Museum, the Sailors' Home, the Cape Town Dispensary and the Ladies' Benevolent Society; £100 to the public libraries of Grahamstown and Port Elizabeth; and £100 to every other public library in the colony at the time of his death.

Porter died on 13 July 1880 in his seventy-fifth year, a week after his brother John Scott. He is buried in the Borough Cemetery, Belfast. When the news reached Cape Town flags were flown at half mast and newspapers throughout the Cape Colony and beyond its boundaries paid tribute to his personal qualities and his public services. All of them stressed the esteem in which he had been held and the dominant position he had occupied.

It is easy enough to understand why, as the *Cape Times* put it, 'no man has ever so gained the affection and admiration of the people of this country',[2] for Porter commended himself to people of all classes and colours. His social equals found him agreeable company. 'Full of Irish wit and humour and charged to the brim with bar anecdotes', he was adept at 'setting the table in a roar' and this without being in the 'least affected by his attention to Baccus'. He would rise from the table at 2 o'clock in the morning 'as if he had merely been indulging in a cup of coffee'.[3] His modesty and indifference to the trappings of power shielded him from jealousy and professional rivalry. His courtesy, consideration and sympathetic interest in others inspired respect and confidence. It is significant that within a few weeks of his arrival the chief justice, Sir John Wylde, confided in him the full story of his wife's desertion and her incest with her son and the false reports of his own incest with his daughter. The same sympathetic interest won him the high regard of his social inferiors, especially since it was accompanied by a readiness to give practical help. He went to great lengths, for example, to see justice done to a drunken Irish emigrant on his way to New South Wales who alleged that he had been maltreated by the ship's captain, even after he had failed to turn up for the dinner to which Porter had invited him and his family.[4] Coloured men who came to his office, often from great distances, were invariably received and had their grievances investigated. His generosity to individuals and to public charities was also well known and widely appreciated.

It is more remarkable that Porter should have dominated Cape affairs to the extent he did, an extent which contemporaries thought worthy of comment. Newspapers far apart physically and politically remarked on it at the time of his death. He was, said the *Natal Mercury*, 'a commanding political figure' whose influence whether in the colonial legislature or at the bar was undisputed: the *Cape Times* stressed 'how powerful was the influence which he brought to bear' and the *Eastern Province Herald* declared that between 1840 and 1865 'perhaps no one had more to do in shaping the politics of the country and his influence was great among his fellow men'.[5]

Yet many of Porter's most cherished beliefs ran counter to the views and prejudices of sections of Cape society. His professional career was dedicated to the administration of equal and impartial justice to the peoples of the colony, regardless of race, religion or language and this often involved upholding the rights of the coloured man against the white man. His conviction that the colony should remain one and undivided conflicted with the aspirations of a good many easterners. His attitude to incursions by blacks from beyond the colony often infuriated the frontier farmers. His championship of the coloured man's political rights was regarded as foolhardy or worse by a lot of white colonists. His latitudinarian approach to religion set him apart from many of his fellow colonists. He had come to the view that:

> Christianity, thank God, is not throughout a thing of controversy. There are many — would there were more — to whom the faith is not a logical system but an animating principle. The soul of Christianity, separated from any particular body of divinity whatever often appears to take up its abode with men of every variety of creed.

He took exception to the form of prayer used at the opening of parliament. Neither parliament nor the executive had any distinctive religion, he said. Jews had sat in the house of assembly and Muslims might in the future and the Christian dogma in the prayer could give offence. He had little patience with those who tried to impose their own moral code on others. A minister who complained about coloured men gambling on Sundays in a private house was urged to consider how hard it would be to draw the line if the law was to take cognizance of the ways in which even professing Christians neglected their Sunday obligations, and another minister was reminded that if a law was made to close canteens at nagmaal as he wished there was no reason why they should not be closed as well on every saint's day in the Roman calendar.[6] Perhaps most startling of all were his views on capital punishment which were shared by few, if any, of his fellow colonists.

It is this very issue of capital punishment, however, which provides the key to an understanding of Porter's position. When J. C. Thompson, member for Grahamstown, tried to have the house counted out while Porter was presenting his bill he incurred the wrath of the *Cape Argus*, not because it approved of the bill but because 'Advocate Thompson fails to grasp the range of Mr Porter's mind or appreciate his character as a man and his position and standing alike in the country and in the house'.[7] The country and the house were prepared to listen to Porter, in spite of his 'odd' opinions on some matters because he was not an odd man. Though some of his pronouncements have a modern ring about them he was not a proto-democrat. He was an early Victorian liberal, applying liberal principles to the problems of his day. So much was he a man of his time that when a volume of his speeches was published only six years after his death, a reviewer declared that it 'introduces us into another world'. As the *Grahamstown Journal* pointed out, his arguments against capital punishment might have been used, and in the editor's opinion more appropriately used, by an English liberal advocating the same cause in England.[8] His concern for justice reflected the liberal's respect for the individual. His liberalism governed his attitude to the colony's non-British peoples. He held the Cape Dutch in high regard, admired the legal system they had bequeathed to the colony and tried to learn their language but his reverence for England as the citadel of freedom convinced him that for them, as for the Irish, it was through English institutions and political ideas that the march of progress could best be assured. His controversial colour-blind franchise was prescribed for a colony which had not yet extended its boundaries to include large numbers of uncivilised blacks. The vast majority of the non-white population were coloured people, a substantial section of whom were showing signs of conforming to European standards of civilisation. He did not envisage the overthrow of the established order of society. Time and time again in the early 1850s he rejected the argument that the coloured man would eventually return sufficient representatives to endanger white ascendancy. What he did believe was that the coloured man should be rewarded for his efforts, and stimulated to greater efforts, to climb the ladder of civilisation.

There were those among his colonial contemporaries who subscribed to the same liberal faith, there were those who respected his basic assumptions while distrusting his specific policies, there were those who accepted his guidance along unfamiliar paths, there were those who out of regard for his character and reputation were prepared to accord him a hearing with tolerance but without being convinced. For one reason or another he had the ear of most of the colonists whose opinions counted, and the confidence of a good many. On the basis of this broad acceptance he established a dominant influence and became 'virtually the mainspring of Cape affairs'.[9]

1   *GTJ*, 21 April 1876; *Address to the University of the Cape of Good Hope by William Porter, chancellor,* Cape Town, 1876.
2   *Cape Times,* quoted in *Eastern Star,* 27 July 1880.
3   Jagger Library, University of Cape Town, Hamilton Ross papers, History of San Souci.
4   Journal, SAL, Porter papers.
5   *Natal Mercury,* 19 July 1880; *Cape Times* quoted in *Eastern Star,* 27 July 1880; *Eastern Province Herald,* 20 July 1880.
6   'The late Hon William Porter', in *South African Law Journal* (1905), xxii. 7; *GTJ*, 28 July 1872; Jagger Library, University of Cape Town, Porter to Rev. Colin Frazer, 3 August 1848; CA, AG 2622, Reports, 1857-9, pp.77.
7   *Argus,* 3 March 1870.
8   *GTJ*, 7 March 1870; Argus, 10 March 1886.
9   *Natal Witness,* 19 August 1880.

Bibliography

A ORIGINAL SOURCES

I   Manuscript Material
South African Library, Cape Town
    Porter papers.
    J. C. Molteno papers.

Cape Archives Depot, Cape Town
    Attorney general's letter books.
    Attorney general's reports.
    Kilpin papers.

University of Cape Town Libraries
    Hamilton Ross papers.
    MS letter Porter to Rev. Colin Frazer, 3 August 1848.

Cory Library, Rhodes University, Grahamstown
    Sprigg papers.
    Roberts papers.

Public Record Office, London
    C.O. 48 Cape. Original correspondence.
    C.O. 49 Entry books.
    C.O. 53 Cape. Miscellanea.
    C.O.336 Cape. Register of correspondence.

Colonial Office Library, London
    Private correspondence of Sir Philip Wodehouse, 1861-9.

Library of Presbyterian Historical Society, Belfast
    MS Fasti of Presbyterian Church.

Manuscripts in private ownership
    Miscellaneous documents relating to the Porter family
    made available by Mrs Margot Vernon, Sir Andrew
    Horsburgh-Porter and Mr Eric Porter.
    Classon papers, made available by Rev. Michael Classon
    MS letter, Frances Porter to Rev. William Porter, 15
    March 1826, made available by Mr Aiken McClelland.

II Printed Material

1 British parliamentary papers

1826-7, H.C., xxi (282) *Inquiry on administration of Cape.*
1827-7, H.C., xii (12) *Second report of commission of Irish education inquiry;* xiii (89) *Fourth report.*
1846, H.C., xxix (400) *Applications for responsible government.*
1849, H.C., xliii (217) *Transport of convicts to Cape.*
1850, H.C.; xxxviii [1137] *Establishment of representative assembly at Cape;* [1138] *Reception of convicts at Cape;* [1234] *Establishment of representative assembly at Cape.*
1851, H.C., xxxvii (457) *Letters patent appointing Sir Harry Smith governor of Cape;* [1362] *Further papers re assembly.*
1852, H.C., xxxiii [1427] *Further papers re assembly.*
1852-3, H.C., lxvi (130) *Petitions re constitution ordinances;* [1581] *Further papers re assembly;* [1636] *Further papers re assembly;* [1640] *Ordinances constituting a parliament.*
1870, H.C., xlix (369) *Establishment of responsible government at Cape;* (181), (181)I, (181)II *Establishment of responsible government at Cape.*
1871, H.C., xlvii [C.459] *Correspondence re affairs of Cape.*
1872, H.C., xviii (286) *Petitions re responsible government.*

2 Cape colony official publications

Minutes of the legislative council and annexures.
Votes and proceedings of the house of assembly with annexures.
Blue-book for the colony of the Cape of Good Hope.
Report of commission on federation, 1872.

3 Newspapers

(a) South African

Cape Argus.
Cape Mercantile Advertiser.
Cape Monitor.
Cape Times.
Eastern Province Herald.
Eastern Star.
Grahamstown Journal, 1832-64, continued as The *Journal.*
The Lantern.
Natal Mercury.

Natal Witness.
South African Commercial Advertiser, 1824-50, continued as
South African Commercial Advertiser and Cape Town Mail to
1856, continued as *South African Advertiser and Mail.*
Standard and Mail.

(b) Irish
Belfast Newsletter.
Dublin Register.
Freeman's Journal.
Londonderry Journal.
Newry Examiner.
Northern Whig.
Ulster Times.

4 Other source material

*A branch of the Porter family. Genealogy compiled by William
Nixon Porter, chiefly from the researches of the late Rev.
Classon Porter, June 1909.*
Cape of Good Hope almanac and annual register.
Dod, *Parliamentary pocket companion for 1838.* London,
1838.
Eybers, G.W., *Select constitutional documents illustrating
South African history, 1795-1910.* London, 1918.
Pigot's Irish directory. 1824.
Slater's Irish directory. 1846.

5 Porter's published works

Under pseudonym 'Laicus', 'Preaching and preachers',
in *The Bible Christian,* v and vi (1834).
*The Porter speeches; speeches delivered by Hon William Porter
during the years 1839-45 inclusive.* Cape Town, 1886.
The public library. Cape Town, 1845.
'O'Connell', in *Cape of Good Hope Literary Magazine* no. 3
(October 1847).
The law of inheritance in the colony of the Cape. Cape Town,
1848.
The elective franchise illustrated and explained. Cape Town,
1853.
*Report of committee on the operation of the law of debtor and
creditor.* Cape Town, (1861?).
The voluntary principle at the Cape. Cape Town, 1869.

Address to the University of the Cape of Good Hope by William Porter, chancellor. Cape Town, 1876.

'Two sonnets', in *Cape Monthly Magazine*, xvi (1879).

B SECONDARY SOURCES

I Books and articles

Benyon, J. *Proconsul and paramountcy in South Africa, 1806-1910.* Pietermaritzburg, 1980

Botha, H.C. *John Fairbairn in South Africa.* Cape Town, 1984.

Boucher, M., *Spes in arduis: a history of the University of South Africa.* Pretoria, 1973; 'The University of the Cape of Good Hope and the University of South Africa, 1873-1946, a study in national and imperial perspectives', in *Archives year book of South African history*, 1972 I.

Breitenbach, J.J. 'Development of secretaryship to government at the Cape of Good Hope under John Montagu, 1845-52', in *Archives year book of South African history*, 1959 II.

Brocker, G. *Rural disorder and police reform in Ireland, 1812-36,* London 1970.

Brown, S.J., *The press in Ireland*, Dublin, 1937.

Challenge and conflict: essays in Irish presbyterian history and doctrine. Antrim, 1981.

Cole, A.W., 'Reminiscences of the Cape bar and Cape bench', in *Cape Law Journal* v (1888); *Reminiscences of my life and of the Cape bench and bar.* Cape Town, 1896.

Crozier, J.A. *Life of Rev. Henry Montgomery.* London, 1875.

Deane, A. (ed) *Belfast Natural History and Philosophical Society centenary volume, 1821-1921.* Belfast, 1924.

Dreyer, E.A. *Jubelfees-gedenkboek van die gemeente Porterville, 1879-1929.* Cape Town, 1930.

Duffy, C.G. *My life in two hemispheres.* London, 1903.

Duminy, A.H. 'Role of Sir Andries Stockenstrom in Cape politics, 1848-54', in *Archives year book of South African history*, 1960 II.

du Toit, A.E., 'The Cape frontier. A study of native policy with special reference to the years 1847-66', in Archives year book of South African history, 1954 I.

Fryer, A.K. 'Government of the Cape of Good Hope, 1825-54: the

140

age of imperial reform', in *Archives year book of South African history*, 1964 I.

Gordon A. and McAlester, C.J. *Memorial addresses and sermons occasioned by the deaths of Rev. John Scott Porter and Hon William Porter*, Belfast, 1880.

Hamilton, G.E. *An account of the Honorable Society of King's Inns, Dublin*. Dublin, 1915.

Hattersley, A.F. *An illustrated social history of South Africa*. Cape Town, 1969; *The convict crisis and the growth of unity*. Pietermaritzburg, 1965; 'Early days of judicial circuits in South Africa', in *Africana Notes and News*, xiii (1958-9).

Immelman, R.F.M. *Men of Good Hope: the romantic story of the Cape Town chamber of commerce, 1804-1954*. Cape Town, 1955.

Inglis, B. *The freedom of the press in Ireland, 1784-1841*. London, 1954.

'The Irish bar, as it was and as it is', in *Dublin University Magazine*, I (1833).

Irwin, C.H. *A history of Presbyterianism in Dublin and the south and west of Ireland*. Dublin, 1890.

Kilpin, R. *The old Cape house*. Cape Town, 1918; *The parliament of the Cape*. London, 1938.

Krauss, F. (ed. Spohr, O.H.) 'A description of Cape Town and its way of life, 1838-40; in *Quarterly Bulletin of South African Library*, xxi (1966-7).

Laidler, P.W. *The growth and government of Cape Town*. Cape Town, 1939.

Laidler, P.W. and Gelfand, M. *South Africa, its medical history, 1652-1898. A medical and social study*. Cape Town, 1971.

Le Cordeur, B.A. 'Robert Godlonton as architect of frontier opinion, 1850-7', in *Archives year book of South African history*, 1942 II; *The politics of Eastern Cape separatism, 1820-1854*. Cape Town, 1981.

Lewson, P. 'The Cape liberal tradition; myth or reality', in *Institute for the study of man in Africa*. Paper No. 26. November 1969.

(ed.) *A Cape traveller's diary, 1856*. By Robert Wilmot Craighall, 1981.

Life at the Cape a hundred years ago. By a lady. Cape Town, 1963.

Limner, L. (R. W. Murray) *Pen and ink sketches in parliament*. Grahamstown, 1864.

Lynar, H. 'In memoriam. To William Porter', in *Cape Monthly Magazine* x (1875).

McDowell, R.B. *Public opinion and government policy in Ireland*, 1801-41. London, 1952.

Marquard, L. *Liberalism in South Africa* Johannesburg, 1965

Martin, T. *Life of the prince consort*, 5 vols London, 1880.

Men of the times. London, 1906.

Midgley, J.F. 'The Orange River Sovereignty (1848-54), in*Archives year book of South African history*

Molteno, P.A. Life and times of Sir John Charles Molteno. 2 vols London, 1900.

Murray, R.W. *South African reminiscences.* Cape Town, 1894.

Norton-Kyshe, J.W. *The law and privileges relating to colonial attorneys general and to the office corresponding to the attorney general of England in the United States of America.* London, 1900.

'Note book of an Irish barrister', in *Metropolitan Magazine*, xxxvii (1843).

C. O'Byrne, *As I roved out.* Belfast, 1946.

O'Flanagan, J.R. *The Irish bar.* London, 1879.

Pama, C. *Wagon road to Wynberg.* Cape Town, 1979.

Peires, J.B., *The dead will arise: Nongquawuse and the great Xhosa cattle-killing movement of 1856-57.* Johannesburg, 1989.

Picard, H.W.J. *Grand Parade: the birth of greater Cape Town.* Cape Town, 1969.

Porter, C. *Irish Presbyterian biographical sketches* Belfast, 1883.

'Hon. William Porter, attorney general', in *Cape Monthly Magazine*, v (1859).

Purves, J. (ed) *Letters from South Africa* by Lady Duff Gordon. London, 1921.

Read, C.A. *Cabinet of Irish literature.* 3 vols, London, 1880.

Richings, F.G. 'The first South African circuits, an early letter', in *South African Law Journal* xc (1973).

Rutherford, J. *Sir George Grey, KCB, 1812-98: a study in colonial government.* London, 1961.

Salmson, V. *My reminiscences.* London, 1926.

Sheil, R.L. *Sketches, legal and political,* 2 vols London, 1855. (ed Savage, M.W.)

Smith, G.H. *The north-east bar. A sketch, historical and reminiscent.* Belfast, 1910.

Solomon, W.E.G. *Saul Solomon, the member for Cape Town.* London, 1948.

Sturgis, J., 'Anglicisation at the Cape of Good Hope in the early nineteenth century,' in *Journal of Imperial and Commonwealth History*, XI (1982).

Tennant, H. *The notary's manual.* 8 vols. Cape Town, 1844.

Trapido, S. 'The origins of the Cape franchise qualification of 1853', in *Journal of African History*, I (1964); ' "The friends of the natives"; merchants, peasants and the political and ideological structure of liberalism in the Cape, 1854-1910', in Marks, S. and Atmore, A. (eds) *Economy and society in pre-industrial South Africa.* London, 1980.

Wilmot, A. *Life and times of Sir Richard Southey.* London, 1904.

    2 Unpublished theses

Kirk, T.E. Self-government and self-defence in South Africa: the inter-relations between British and Cape politics, 1846-54. D. Phil thesis, University of Oxford

Putzel, J.R. William Porter and constitutional issues at the Cape, 1839-72. M.A. thesis, University of Cape Town, 1942

Sole, D.B. The separation movement and the demand for resident government in the Eastern Province. M.A. thesis, Rhodes University, Grahamstown, 1939

Taylor, N.H. The separation movement during the period of representative government at the Cape, 1854-72. M.A. thesis, University of Cape Town, 1938

Trapido, S. White conflict and non-white participation in the politics of the Cape of Good Hope, 1853-1910. Ph.D. thesis, University of London, 1970

Zeeman, M.J. The working of representative government at the Cape under Sir P. Wodehouse, 1862-70. M.A. thesis, University of Cape Town, 1940

Glossary

Arianism

Doctrine propounded by Arius of Alexandria in the fourth century denying that Christ was consubstantial with God. It found favour with some Irish presbyterians.

Catholic emancipation

The freeing of catholics from the last vestiges of the penal code, notably their exclusion from parliament. O'Connell's campaign mobilized catholic opinion as never before but is also aroused sectarian bitterness.

New Light party

A minority group within the presbyterian church who held various heterodox doctrines on the Trinity and opposed a too rigid definition of belief. In politics, as in theology, they took a liberal stand, supporting such causes as catholic emancipation. They were eventually forced to secede.

Old Light Party

The orthodox majority in the presbyterian church who demanded subscription to the 1643 Westminster Confession of Faith, were strongly evangelical and were conservative in their political allegiance.

Orangemen

Members of the Orange Order, a protestant secret society founded at the end of the eighteenth century at a time of agrarian and sectarian conflict between protestant and catholic peasants in Ulster. It has survived as a fervant upholder of protestantism, the British connection and the British constitution.

Plantation of Ulster

After the flight of the native Irish chiefs from Ulster to Europe in 1607 their lands were con-

144

fiscated and a scheme to colonise them with settlers from England and Scotland was drawn up by the English government for six of the newly created Ulster counties. The city of London was made responsible for one of them, hence the renaming of Derry as Londonderry in 1613. Other parts of Ulster were colonised by private enterprise at the same time.

Ribbonmen Members of a secret society in nineteenth- century Ireland with nationalist aspirations but primarily concerned with the redress of social and economic grievances by violent means. The term was loosely used to describe the many agrarian secret societies among the catholic peasantry.

Townland The smallest and oldest division of land in Ireland; townlands pre-date the division of the country into counties on the model of the English shires. There are over 60,000 of them, varying considerably in size.

United Irishmen A Society founded in Ireland in 1791 inspired by the ideals of the French Revolution. Faced by the government's intransigence it became a secret society plotting rebellion with French help. The rebellion in 1798 was confined to limited areas and was fuelled as much by sectarian passions and agrarian grievances as by political idealism.

Young Irelanders A group of young, mainly middle class, intellectuals within O'Connell's movement for the repeal of the union between Britain and Ireland which became increasingly disillusioned with O'Connell's views and methods. Their objection in particular to his dependence on the catholic church and his renunciation of force eventually led to a breach and, in 1848, to a futile attempt at rebellion.

145

Boer   A farmer whose roots went back to the days of Dutch colony. The name came to be applied to all such people as an alternative to Africander. With the development of Afrikaans as a distinct language Afrikaner became normal.

Cattle killing of 1857   A millenarian movement among the Xhosa people beyond the eastern frontier of the Cape Colony. Following a prophecy by a sixteen year old girl they slaughtered their cattle and destroyed their crops in expectation of a miraculous replacement of cattle and corn and a mighty wind which would sweep the white man into the sea. The outcome was mass starvation and a great influx of Xhosa into the colony.

Drostdy   Office and residence of the landdrost or chief magistrate of a district in the Dutch colony at the Cape.

Field cornet   A local official with civil, judicial and military functions selected from among the farmers in the district for which he was responsible.

Field commandant   Another farmer-official, in charge of the local commando (militia).

Fiscal   An official at the Cape under the Dutch regime concerned with law enforcement and the revenue. The office survived under the British until 1827 when the fiscal was replaced by an attorney general. The awe in which the fiscal was held is reflected in the name given to a South African bird, the fiscal shrike, which is given to impaling its prey on thorns. An alterative popular name for it is Jacky Hangman.

Great Trek   The movement northwards from the Cape Colony of many disgruntled and land-hungry pre-

146

British colonists from 1836 onwards. It led eventually to the founding of the two independent Boer republics, the Orange Free State and the South African Republic.

Griqua   A people of mixed race from the western Cape who had moved by Porter's day to the region of the middle Orange and Transorangia. They had originally called themselves Bastards but the London Missionary Society persuaded then to adopt the name Griqua after a Hottentot or Khoikhoi tribe, one of their components.

Hottentots/Khoikhoi   In Porter's day and for nearly a hundred years
Bushmen/San   after the peoples whom the Dutch found at the Cape when they had arrived in the seventeenth century were called Hottentots and Bushmen. Then the names were changed to Khoikhoi and San or, since the differences between them were less than once believed, collectively to Khoisan.

Index

Bulwer-Lytton, Sir Edward, 113
Burgersdorp, 98
Bushmanland, 98
Bushmen, *see* San

Caldwell, Dr, 22
Camperdown, 76
Cambrian, 77
Canada, 117, 118
Cape Argus, 69, 134
Cape Colony, 55, 59-63, 67, 68, 79, 86, 88, 89, 91, 95, 96, 97, 99, 100, 103, 105, 116, 117, 118, 119, 121, 123, 124, 125, 132, 134, 147
Cape Commercial Bank, 76
Cape Dutch, 76, 77, 123, 135
Cape Hunt, 72
Cape Mounted Police, 99, 100
Cape of Good Hope Agricultural Society, 75
Cape of Good Hope Bank, 62
Cape of Good Hope Gas Light Company, 76
Cape of Good Hope Humane Society, 75
Cape of Good Hope Savings Bank, 75
Cape parliament, 67, 68, 92, 96, 119, 120, 122-127, 134
  See also House of assembly
  and Legislative council
Cape Times, 132, 133
Cape Town, 54, 59, 61-67, 68, 69, 71-77, 79, 82, 85, 95, 107, 114, 115, 117, 118, 119, 123, 125, 131, 132
Cape Town Dispensary, 76, 132
Cape Town volunteer cavalry, 75, 76
Cape volunteers, 70, 75, 76
Capital punishment 91, 127, 134, 135
Carrickfergus, 21
Catholic Association, 29
Catholic emancipation, 26, 27, 29, 30, 35, 36, 119, 144
Catholics, in Ireland, 25, 26, 41, 42
Cattle killing, 1857, 110, 116, 146
Chamberlain, Joseph, 47
Church of England Provident Society, 75
Church of Ireland, 18, 20, 25, 26, 28
Clanwilliam, 77
Classon and Duggan, 23
Classon family, 21, 23

Mitchel, John, 40, 46
Molteno, J.C., 125, 126
Monaghan (town), 33
Montagu, John, 62, 74, 93, 106, 124
Montgomery, Rev. Henry, 30, 38
Moore, Rev. William, 28
Morning Register, 45
Moshweshwe, 102, 110
Mowbray, 69
Mulgrave, *see* Normanby
Munster, Synod of, 31
Murphy, Patrick Matthias, 41
Musgrave, (acting attorney general), 79, 114

Namaqualand, 98
Napier, Sir George, 71, 85, 90
Napier, Lady, 71
Natal,59, 85, 99, 108, 116
Natal, Mercury, 133
Nelson, Joseph, 41
New Light, 20, 21, 30, 31, 34, 42, 97, 144
Newry Examiner, 42
Newtownlimavady, *see* Limavady
Newtownmountkennedy, 22
Nixon, (greatgrandfather of W.P.), 20
Nixon, Jane *see* Porter, Jane
Non-Subscribing Presbyterians, Association of, 31
Normanby, Constantine Henry Phipps, 3rd marquess of 44, 45, 47
Northern Whig, 21, 27, 35, 42, 73
Northumberland Hotel, Dublin, 23

O'Connell, Daniel, 29, 34-36, 38, 41, 42
O'Connell, Morgan John, 48
O'Hagan, Rev. Edward, 43
Old Light, 30, 144
Oliphant, Anthony, 40, 41, 45, 79, 82, 114
O'Loghlen, Michael, 42, 47
Omagh, 18, 33
Orange Free State, 59, 87, 147
Orange Order, 26, 42, 73, 144
Orange river, 62, 101, 103
Orange River Sovereignty, 108, 116

Orthodox Presbyterian, 34

Pakington, Sir John, 105
Palmerston, Co. Dublin, 22
Palmerston, Henry John Temple, 3rd Viscount, 90
Paris Exhibition of 1854, 75
Patriotic Fund, 74, 75
Parliament, Cape *see* Cape parliament
Perrin, Louis, 40, 47
Philip, Dr John, 72, 102
Philippolis, 102, 103
Phillips, Sir Thomas, 17
Pigot, David Richard, 40, 47, 48
Plunket, William Conyngham, 1st Baron, 40
Port Elizabeth, 82, 84, 132
Porter family, 17, 18, 29
Porter, Rev. Classon (half-brother of W.P.), 21, 28, 44
Porter (née Classon), Eliza (stepmother of W.P.), 17, 22, 23, 28, 73
Porter, Francis (half-brother of W.P.) 21, 70, 72, 73, 89, 131
Porter, James (uncle of W.P.), 20
Porter, Rev. James (of Greyabbey), 29
Porter, Rev. James Nixon (half-brother of W.P.), 21
Porter, (née Nixon), Jane (grandmother of W.P.), 18
Porter, John (grandfather of W.P.), 18, 19
Porter, Rev. John Scott (brother of W.P.), 21, 28, 28, 31-34, 72, 90, 131, 132
Porter, (née Scott), Mary (mother of W.P.), 17, 19, 22, 23, 28.
Porter, Mary Eliza (niece of W.P.), 131
Porter, William
    Neglected by biographers, 8
    His liberalism, 9, 10, 35-37, 133-136
    Birth, 17
    Family background, 17-21
    Childhood and schooling, 28, 29
    Apprenticeship to uncle, 29, 31
    Aunt suggests legal career, 31
    Legal training, 32
    Early career at bar, 32, 33, 38
    Religious opinions, 33-35, 68, 72, 134
    Attitudes to Catholic emancipation and repeal of the Act of Union, 35-37
    Appointed as attorney general of Cape, 40-43

San, 60, 98, 100, 147
Sarhili, 110
Scott, John (grandfather of W.P.), 19
Scott, Mary *see* Porter, Mary
1798 rebellion, 19, 20, 25, 28, 29, 39
Sheep, 62, 82
Slaves and slavery, 61, 64, 99
Smith, Eliza, 70
Smith, Sir Harry, 119
Smith, Mr, passenger on *Sterling*, 50, 52
Solomon, Saul, 66, 126
Somerset East, 82, 83, 85, 93
Sotho, 101, 102
South African Bank, 62
South African College, 75
South African Commercial Advertiser, 102
South African Infant Schools, 75
South African Literary and Scientific Institution, 75
South African Public Library, 75, 76, 132
Stanbridge, passenger on *Sterling*, 50, 53
Stanley, Edward Geoffrey Smith, Lord, later 14th earl of Derby, 118, 119
Starving Irish Committee, 74
Stellenbosch, 82
Stephen, James, 45
Stephenson, James, 28
Sterling, 44, 49, 73
Stockenstrom, Sir Andries, 85, 93
Strabane, presbytery of, 19
Swart (employer of servant girl), 99
Swellendam, 82, 84, 86
Syme, passenger on *Sterling*, 50

Table bay, 54, 75
Table Mountain, 54, 64
Tennant, Hercules, 92
Thembu, 100, 101
Thompson, J.C., 134, 135
Thomson (missionary), 102
Ticket-of-leave men, at Cape, 117, 118
Tipperary, Co., 42
Touwfontein, 103

Townshend, passenger on *Sterling*, 50
Transorangia, 103, 108, 116, 147
Transvaal, 59
Tyrone, Co., 18

Uitenhage, 82, 84, 85,88, 98, 100
Ulster Times, 43
Unitarianism, 20, 21, 30, 33, 34, 37, 45, 72
     see also Remonstrant Synod of Ulster
United Irishmen, 19, 22, 145
University of the Cape of Good Hope, 75, 131, 132

Van den Linden (legal author), 52, 81
Van der Byl family, 64
Van der Walt family, 83
Van Rensbergh family, 84
Van Ryneveld (advocate), 83, 84
Venning (merchant), 72
Victoria, Queen, 47, 48
Volunteers (Cape),
     see Cape Town volunteer cavalry
     and Cape volunteers
Volunteers (Irish)
     see Lawyers' corps of volunteers
     and Limavady corps of volunteers

Wakefield, Edward Gibbon, 117
Walker, Robert, 33
Warrington, 21
Waterboer (Griqua captain), 101, 102
Watermeyer, Mr Justice, E.B., 91
Wicklow, Co., 21, 22
Witchcraft, 101
Wodehouse, Sir Philip, 91, 116, 125
Wolfe, Captain, R.T., 9
Wood (member of Cape legislative council), 92
Wood, Sir Charles, 106
Worcester, 98
Woulfe, Stephen, 46
Wylde, Edward, 83
Wylde, Sir John, 72, 80-84, 90, 93, 133

Xhosa, 60, 110, 146